AF473752

Markus Raetz
Zeemansblik

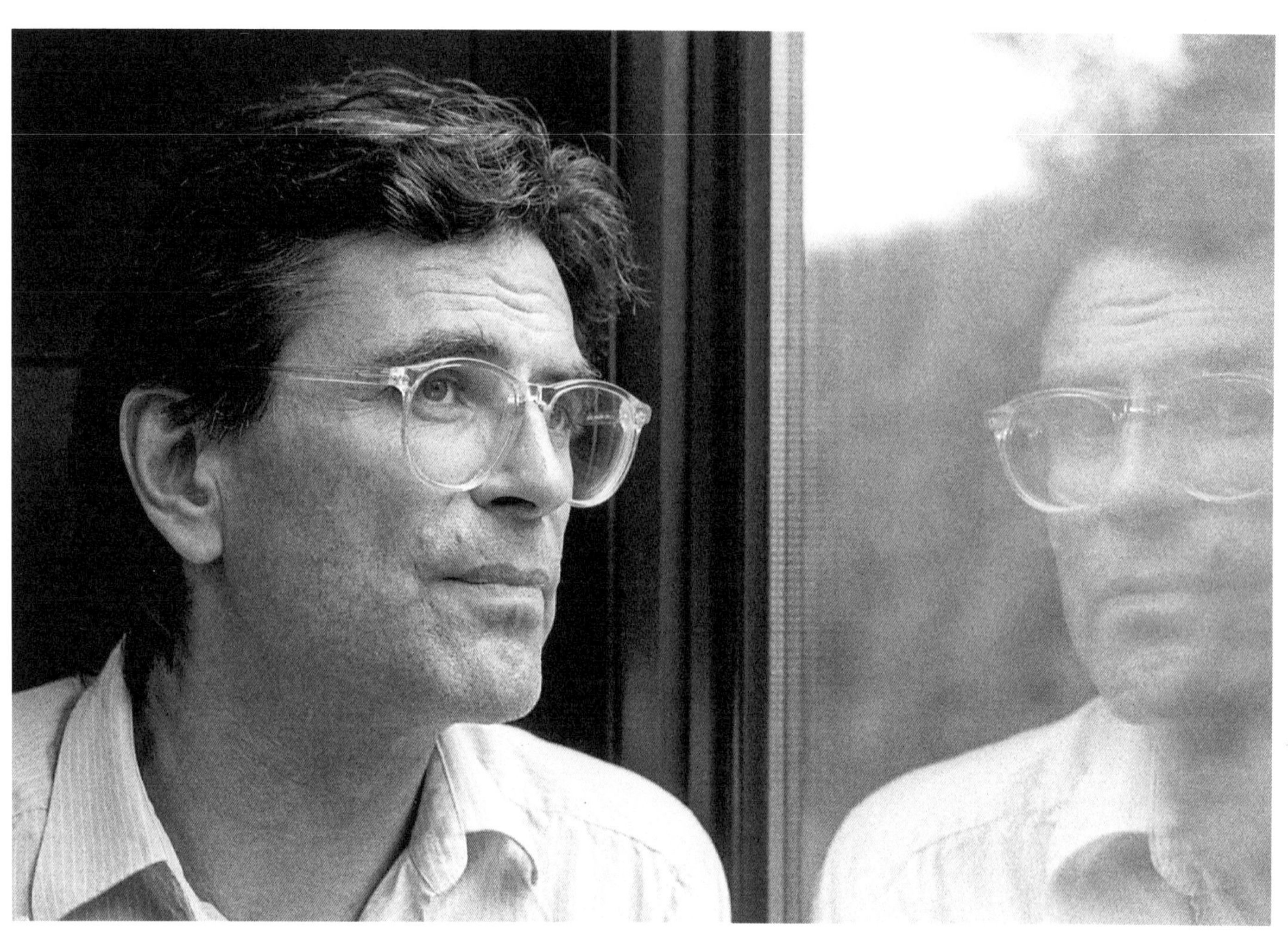

Franz Müller

Markus Raetz
Zeemansblik

Scheidegger & Spiess

Editor's Foreword

The seventh volume in the Landmarks of Swiss Art series is devoted to the work *Zeemansblik* by Markus Raetz.

Markus Raetz (1941–2020) was an explorer of seeing. He understood seeing as movement, as a process, and as a constantly fresh adventure. The theme of seeing, or more accurately of perception, is a key strand of his art. It is illustrated in exemplary fashion in his landmark work *Zeemansblik* from 1987.

Now housed at the Aargauer Kunsthaus in Aarau, *Zeemansblik* entered the collection in 2000. Measuring 83 centimeters in height and 134 centimeters in width, it is the largest of a whole series of works with the same title, created between 1985 and 1999 in various dimensions.

As project leader and co-author of the catalogue raisonné of Markus Raetz's sculptural œuvre, published in 2023, Franz Müller is ideally qualified to investigate *Zeemansblik* in terms of its artistic evolution and role within Raetz's body of work as a whole. Müller's fascinating research reveals the complexity of this landmark piece. *Zeemansblik* captivates with its stringency and reduction, and at the same time engages us in a confusing and multilayered play with perception. Like René Magritte before him, Raetz, too, mistrusted the extent to which what we see with our eyes is actually real. *Zeemansblik* is both conceptual and addressed to the senses.

The *Zeemansblik* work group was inspired in equal measure by the Netherlands, where Markus Raetz lived and worked from 1969 to 1973 in a fruitful phase of his artistic career, and by the south of France, where he regularly spent time for many years. In these areas of Europe, the ocean is never far away. And who doesn't love a sea vista? A sweeping view into the far distance, divided only by the horizon line into a below and an above, into water and sky. A view that was already sought out by the Romanticists and which expressed their yearning for the unknown yonder and the infinite. Raetz was certainly not unfamiliar with this Romantic sense of longing and possibly considered it to be an allusion in his work. But he also assigned the view of the sea, in an entirely sober and pragmatic way, to the *Zeeman*, the sailor or seafarer, whom he provides with a suitable counterpart in the figure of the *Feldstechermann*—the sculpture of a man looking through field glasses, standing on top of a tall plinth. The binocular shape of the field glasses forms the silhouette of the relief *Zeemansblik*, which is conceived as a kind of field of view. Its curving outline encloses shim-

Vorwort der Herausgeberin

Der siebte Band in der Reihe *Schlüsselwerke der Schweizer Kunst* ist der Arbeit *Zeemansblik* von Markus Raetz gewidmet.

Markus Raetz (1941–2020) war ein Erforscher des Sehens. Er verstand das Sehen als Bewegung, als einen Prozess und als immer wieder neues Abenteuer. Das Thema des Sehens oder besser des Wahrnehmens steht im Zentrum seines Schaffens. Es lässt sich exemplarisch am Schlüsselwerk *Zeemansblik* (1987) festmachen.

Das 83 Zentimeter hohe und 134 Zentimeter breite Werk befindet sich seit dem Jahr 2000 im Aargauer Kunsthaus in Aarau. Es ist das grösste einer ganzen Reihe gleichnamiger, zwischen 1985 und 1999 entstandener Arbeiten in verschiedenen Dimensionen.

Franz Müller ist als Projektleiter und Mitautor des 2023 erschienenen *Catalogue raisonné* des plastischen Schaffens von Markus Raetz geradezu prädestiniert, dem Schlüsselwerk *Zeemansblik* in seiner künstlerischen Entwicklung und Rolle innerhalb des gesamten Œuvres nachzugehen. Seine spannenden Recherchen legen die Komplexität dieses Werkes offen. Es besticht durch seine Stringenz und Reduktion und lädt uns gleichzeitig zu einem verwirrenden und vielschichtigen Spiel mit der Wahrnehmung ein. In der Nachfolge René Magrittes stehend, misstraute auch Raetz dem Realitätsgehalt des konstatierenden Sehens. Das Werk ist genauso konzeptuell wie sinnlich angelegt.

Zeemansblik ist gleichermassen von den Niederlanden, wo Markus Raetz von 1969 bis 1973 eine fruchtbare Arbeitsphase erlebte, wie von Südfrankreich inspiriert, wo er sich über viele Jahre hinweg regelmässig aufhielt. In diesen Ländern ist die Nähe des Meeres omnipräsent und der Blick darauf leicht möglich. Wer liebt ihn nicht? Den Blick in die Weite, die nur durch die Horizontlinie in ein Unten und ein Oben, in Wasser und Himmel unterteilt wird. Ein Blick, der schon den Romantikern vertraut war und ihre Sehnsucht nach unbekannter Ferne, ja Unendlichkeit, zum Ausdruck brachte. Nicht dass Raetz dieses Empfinden fremd gewesen wäre und er die Anspielung darauf nicht mitbedacht hätte. Er weist den Blick auf das Meer aber auch ganz nüchtern und pragmatisch dem Seefahrer bzw. dem Matrosen zu. Diesem hat er mit dem auf einem hohen Sockel stehenden *Feldstechermann* ein passendes Pendant beigegeben. Die bipolare Rundform des Feldstechers bildet die Silhouette vom Werk *Zeemansblik*, das als eine Art Sehfeld aufgefasst ist. Die beiden Rundungen umschliessen sanft abgestufte,

mering surfaces flowing gently and smoothly one into the other, suggesting the sea and the sky. The color mood shifts with every step we take towards or away from the work, making us aware of how changeable and approximate seeing is. The atmosphere of the image changes, at times appearing brighter and more cheerful, and then growing gloomier again.

The word *blik* in Dutch not only means view, but also sheet metal. This material served Markus Raetz as a support for *Zeemansblik*. In our perception, the fold below the middle of the zinc sheet appears as a horizon line. Condensing the shape, material, and content of the work into its title, the artist once again points to the ambiguity of seeing.

In his essay, Franz Müller examines the different variations of *Zeemansblik* and looks at the drawings and paintings that paved the way towards it. The motifs of the head, eye, and pyramid of vision appear early on in Raetz's work. The movement of seeing is later channeled and focused through caves or holes in rocks. From there, it is only a short step to the binocular view through field glasses.

Zeemansblik connects drawing, painting, and sculpture in an installation that incorporates us as viewers, and in which we can observe the *Feldstechermann* observing.

The author and the editor wish to thank Monika Rätz, who carefully oversees the estate of Markus Raetz. She welcomed our project warmly from the very beginning and facilitated our work in every way.

Angelika Affentranger-Kirchrath

ineinander übergehende schimmernde Flächen, die Meer und Himmel andeuten. Die farbige Gestimmtheit ändert sich mit jedem Schritt des Betrachters auf das Werk zu oder von ihm weg und macht bewusst, wie wandelbar und ungefähr das Sehen ist. Die Bildatmosphäre changiert, scheint einmal heiterer, dann wieder verdüstert.

Blik bedeutet auf Holländisch nicht nur Blick, sondern auch Blech. Ein solches diente Markus Raetz als Bildträger. Der Falz unterhalb der Mitte des Zinkblechs erscheint in unserer Wahrnehmung als Horizontlinie. Schon im Titel des Werks führt der Künstler Form, Material und Inhalt zusammen und verweist damit einmal mehr auf die Ambiguität des Sehens.

Franz Müller zeigt in seiner Abhandlung die Variationsbreite des Werkes auf. Dazu gehören auch die vielen Vorgängerarbeiten in der Form von Zeichnungen und Bildern. Früh tauchen die Motive Kopf, Auge und Sehpyramide in Markus Raetz' Schaffen auf. Später wird die Bewegung des Sehens durch Höhlen oder Felsenlöcher kanalisiert und fokussiert. Von da aus ist der Schritt zum Blick durch den Feldstecher nicht mehr weit.

Zeemansblik verbindet Zeichnung, Malerei und Plastik in einer Rauminstallation. Indem sie uns als Betrachterinnen und Betrachter mit einschliesst, können wir den *Feldstechermann* beim Beobachten beobachten.

Der Autor und die Herausgeberin danken Monika Rätz, die den Nachlass von Markus Raetz mit Umsicht betreut. Von Anfang an begegnete sie unserem Projekt mit grossem Wohlwollen und unterstützte die Arbeit daran in jeder Hinsicht.

Angelika Affentranger-Kirchrath

Franz Müller

Markus Raetz: *Zeemansblik*

Markus Raetz: An Outstanding Representative of Post-war Modernism

"The emptiness of these metal sheets is infinitely vast."[1] In 1989, Dieter Koepplin, the then head of the Basel Kupferstichkabinett, curated an exhibition of Markus Raetz's works at the Museum für Gegenwartskunst in Basel. With this one brief sentence, he summed up the impression conveyed by a number of works at the center of the show. They formed part of a series of sheet-metal reliefs with the silhouette of two circular discs of the same size, side by side and overlapping, and a continuous horizontal fold. All bear the title *Zeemansblik*.[2]

At the end of the 1980s, Markus Raetz (1941–2020) was already a successful artist and an established figure in the art world.[3] He had taken part in outstanding manifestations of contemporary art, such as the 1968, 1972, and 1982 editions of documenta in Kassel, and the 43rd Venice Biennale in 1988, when he occupied the Swiss pavilion. Between 1964 and 1989, he took part in some seventy solo shows and presentations of larger work groups, both in commercial art galleries and renowned museums in Switzerland, as well in other parts of Europe and the United States. A first highlight of his exhibition career came in 1977 with his parallel shows at the Kunstmuseum Bern and the Kunsthalle Bern—an honor that has been bestowed on very few artists to date. Taking into account all the thematic exhibitions in which he participated during this same period, the total adds up to almost a further 300 appearances. It seems evident that he was represented at practically every exhibition abroad offering insights into contemporary Swiss art. The literature published about him during this time is correspondingly extensive. From the 1990s on, Raetz exhibited even more intensively, with some sixty, mostly wide-ranging, presentations of his work staged in venues from Aarau and Basel to Antwerp, Helsinki, Milan, Lisbon, Paris, New York, and San Francisco. Many of these shows were accompanied by extensive monographs featuring in-depth essays. On top of this solo activity, Raetz also participated in over 400 exhibitions on a very wide spectrum of themes. At the start of the early 2000s, a documentary movie was made about him, and in 2005 more than ninety texts written about his work between 1967 and 2005 were published as a compendium.[4] The catalogues raisonnés of his prints and sculptures were published in 2014 and 2023 respectively. Raetz achieved classic status during his own lifetime as a representative of post-war modernism.

Franz Müller

Markus Raetz: *Zeemansblik*

Markus Raetz: Klassiker der Nachkriegsmoderne

«Das Nichts dieser Bleche ist unendlich viel.» Mit einem knappen Satz umriss Dieter Koepplin, der Leiter des Basler Kupferstichkabinetts, die Wirkung einiger Werke, die 1989 im Zentrum einer von ihm kuratierten Ausstellung von Markus Raetz im Museum für Gegenwartskunst in Basel standen.[1] Sie gehörten zu einer Reihe von Reliefs aus Blech mit der Silhouette zweier gleich grosser, nebeneinander angeordneter und sich überlappender Kreisscheiben und einem durchlaufenden horizontalen Falz. Alle tragen den Titel *Zeemansblik*.[2]

Markus Raetz (1941–2020) war damals, Ende der 1980er Jahre, ein im Kunstbetrieb anerkannter und erfolgreicher Künstler.[3] Er hatte an herausragenden Manifestationen der Gegenwartskunst teilgenommen, so 1968, 1972 und 1982 an der documenta in Kassel und 1988 an der 43. Biennale von Venedig, wo er den Schweizer Pavillon bespielte. Von 1964 bis 1989 erhielt er gut 70 Einzelausstellungen oder Präsentationen grösserer Werkgruppen in der Schweiz, in mehreren europäischen Ländern und in den USA, sowohl in Galerien als auch in renommierten Museen. Einen ersten Höhepunkt seiner Ausstellungskarriere bildeten 1977 die parallelen Schauen im Kunstmuseum Bern und in der Kunsthalle Bern, eine Ehre, die wohl bis heute nur sehr wenigen Kunstschaffenden zuteilwurde. Berücksichtigt man ausserdem alle Beteiligungen an thematischen Ausstellungen, kommen im genannten Zeitraum fast 300 weitere Auftritte hinzu. Dass er an praktisch allen Ausstellungen, die im Ausland Einblicke in die Schweizer Gegenwartskunst boten, vertreten war, scheint selbstverständlich. Entsprechend umfangreich ist die Literatur, die in dieser Zeit über ihn erschien. Ab den 1990er Jahren entfaltete Raetz eine noch intensivere Ausstellungstätigkeit. Zu den rund 60, meist breit angelegten Werkpräsentationen von Aarau und Basel über Antwerpen, Helsinki, Mailand, Lissabon und Paris bis New York und San Francisco erschienen oft umfangreiche Monografien mit ausführlichen Essays. Dazu kamen über 400 Beteiligungen an Ausstellungen mit einem sehr weit gefassten thematischen Spektrum. Anfang der 2000er Jahre wurde ein Dokumentarfilm über ihn gedreht, 2005 erschien ein Kompendium mit mehr als 90 in den Jahren 1967 bis 2005 über ihn verfassten Texten,[4] und 2014 bzw. 2023 wurden die Werkverzeichnisse der Druckgrafiken und des plastischen Œuvres herausgegeben. Raetz erreichte noch zu Lebzeiten den Status eines Klassikers der Nachkriegsmoderne.

In 1989, Markus Raetz was already able to look back on almost thirty years of artistic production. In the stimulating environment of the Bern art scene around the young Kunsthalle director Harald Szeemann, the self-taught Raetz had immediately forged connections with current international trends. While his earliest drawings and paintings remained oriented towards avant-garde art of the 1950s, from the mid-1960s on he absorbed ideas from Concrete Art, Op Art, and Pop Art. Linked to this was his shift from painting to sculpture, or more accurately the fluctuating position of his works between the genres of visual art—something that would characterize his entire subsequent œuvre. In the late 1960s, Raetz began to explore conceptual approaches: in 1969 he was represented at the important exhibition *Live in Your Head: When Attitudes Become Form* at the Kunsthalle Bern and in 1970 at the show *Visualisierte Denkprozesse* at the Kunstmuseum Lucerne. In Amsterdam, where he lived from 1969 to 1973, he devoted himself to printmaking and above all to drawing, which formed the enduring basis of his entire œuvre and offered a seemingly inexhaustible reservoir of ideas. In 1976, after three years in the village of Carona in Ticino, he returned to Bern, which now became the birthplace of an extraordinarily multifaceted sculptural œuvre, in which movement, metamorphosis, and the exposure of clarity as a precarious, only ever temporary state, are crucial. The field of allusions, quotations, paraphrases, and homages, and of references to art history, literature, and daily life, is immeasurably vast. It is the combined expression of Raetz's great knowledge, humor, and sensitive feel for what is seemingly unconnected and remote that reveals a new poetic dimension and possesses its own logic—as in the landmark *Zeemansblik*.

The *Zeemansblik* Work Group and Its Reception

The *Zeemansblik* work group comprises seventeen reliefs created between 1985 and 1999. The smallest measures 21 cm across, and the largest 134 cm (fig. 1).[5] In addition to the versions numbered by the artist, the group also includes several smaller examples around only 10 cm wide.[6] Although the same in terms of shape, these differ from the others in their material: they are made of tinplate from empty tins of instant coffee, whereas for the larger versions Raetz used zinc sheets. In many cases these are cliché (printing) plates, which Raetz cut into the desired shape for his reliefs.[7] He also reserved two corre-

Markus Raetz konnte 1989 schon auf ein knapp 30-jähriges Schaffen zurückblicken. Der Autodidakt hatte im anregenden Umfeld der Berner Kunstszene um den jungen Kunsthalle-Direktor Harald Szeemann sofort Anschluss an die aktuellen internationalen Tendenzen gefunden. Seine frühesten grafischen und malerischen Werke hatten sich noch an avantgardistischen Positionen der 1950er Jahre orientiert. Ab Mitte der 1960er Jahre nahm er Anregungen der konkreten Kunst, der Op-Art, und der Pop-Art auf. Damit verbunden war der Übergang von der Malerei zur Skulptur bzw. die fluktuierende Position der Werke zwischen den bildkünstlerischen Gattungen, die sein ganzes weiteres Schaffen prägte. Ende der 1960er Jahre wandte sich Raetz konzeptuellen Ansätzen zu und war 1969 an der bedeutenden Ausstellung *Live in Your Head: When Attitudes Become Form* in der Berner Kunsthalle und 1970 in der Schau *Visualisierte Denkprozesse* im Kunstmuseum Luzern vertreten. Während seines von 1969 bis 1973 dauernden Aufenthaltes in Amsterdam widmete er sich der Druckgrafik und vor allem der Zeichnung, die seit jeher die Grundlage und das unerschöpflich anmutende Ideenreservoir seines gesamten Schaffens bildete. Nach drei Jahren im Tessiner Dorf Carona kehrte Raetz 1976 nach Bern zurück, wo ein ausserordentlich vielfältiges skulpturales Werk seinen Ausgang nahm. Darin sind Bewegung und Verwandlung, die Entlarvung von Eindeutigkeit als einem prekären, stets nur vorläufigen Zustand wesentlich. Das Feld der verarbeiteten kunsthistorischen, literarischen und lebensweltlichen Bezüge, der Anspielungen, Zitate, Paraphrasen, Referenzen und Reverenzen ist unüberblickbar weit. Es ist Ausdruck von Raetz' grossem Wissen, seinem Humor und seiner Sensibilität für scheinbar Unzusammenhängendes und Entlegenes, das zusammengeführt eine neue poetische Dimension offenbart und seine eigene Logik besitzt – wie im Schlüsselwerk *Zeemansblik*.

Die Werkgruppe *Zeemansblik* und ihre Rezeption

Die Werkgruppe *Zeemansblik* umfasst 17 Reliefs, die in den Jahren 1985 bis 1999 entstanden. Das kleinste misst in der waagrechten Ausdehnung 21 Zentimeter und das grösste 134 Zentimeter (Abb. 1).[5] Ausserhalb der von ihm nummerierten Versionen schuf Raetz eine Anzahl kleinerer, nur rund zehn Zentimeter breiter Exemplare.[6] Sie unterscheiden sich von den übrigen nicht in der Form, sondern hinsichtlich des Materials; sie bestehen aus dem Weissblech von ausrangierten

1
Zeemansblik, 1987
Zinkblech, gefalzt, rückseitige Aufhängevorrichtung: Holz / Zinc sheet, folded, rear-mounted hanging fixture:
wood, 83 × 134 × 4,4 cm, 0,1 cm (Stärke Blech / sheet thickness)
Aargauer Kunsthaus, Aarau

spondingly trimmed plates for etchings, of which he used one for his 1986 drypoint *Sehfeld* (fig. 2).[8] The second plate was never used for printmaking and ten years later became the small *Zeemansblik* number 16 (fig. 3).[9] In February 1987, Raetz bought two sheets of titanium zinc, each measuring 100 × 200 cm, in the thicknesses 0.7 mm and 1 mm.[10] He chose this material, which is mainly used for façades, roofs, and gutters, for the two largest versions of *Zeemansblik*. Today both are housed in museums.[11]

The very largest version, number 11 in the series, belongs to the Aargauer Kunsthaus in Aarau and was acquired for its collection in 2000. It was made in March 1987.[12] Versions 9 and 10 were also created in 1987 and are both dated to the beginning of March. Numbers 1 to 8, comprising the first half of the group, were produced between July 1985 and July 1986. Numbers 12 to 15 date from 1988. After a lengthy gap, version 16 followed in 1996 and finally 17 in 1999.

Markus Raetz treated certain works occupying a pivotal role in his œuvre in multiple variations, in some cases over a long period of time. The substantial number of *Zeemansblik* reliefs he produced over the course of almost one and a half decades is therefore cogent evidence of the importance of this series. In contrast to other major works, however, it is striking that the individual versions differ almost solely, albeit considerably, in terms of their size, while varying only very slightly in terms of material and form.[13] Sheet metal as a material, and the characteristic shape of the coupled circular discs, were firmly established with *Zeemansblik* number 1 and required no further optimization. Any variation would probably have rendered the artist's statement less clear, rather than building upon it.[14] Even Raetz's later adaptations of the motif in his prints remained remarkably faithful to the appearance of the reliefs.[15] The importance of *Zeemansblik* is most evident in the fact that, from 1986 onwards, the relief—in particular the larger versions—featured in the vast majority of exhibitions at which Raetz was represented with extensive groups of works. The large Aarau version has been shown most frequently of all: it is documented in some twenty exhibitions between 1993 and 2023. Many of these exhibitions were representative overviews of Raetz's œuvre, inconceivable without the presence of a *Zeemansblik*. In other cases, a *Zeemansblik* has been included in exhibitions in particularly celebrated venues, as for example in 1988 at the

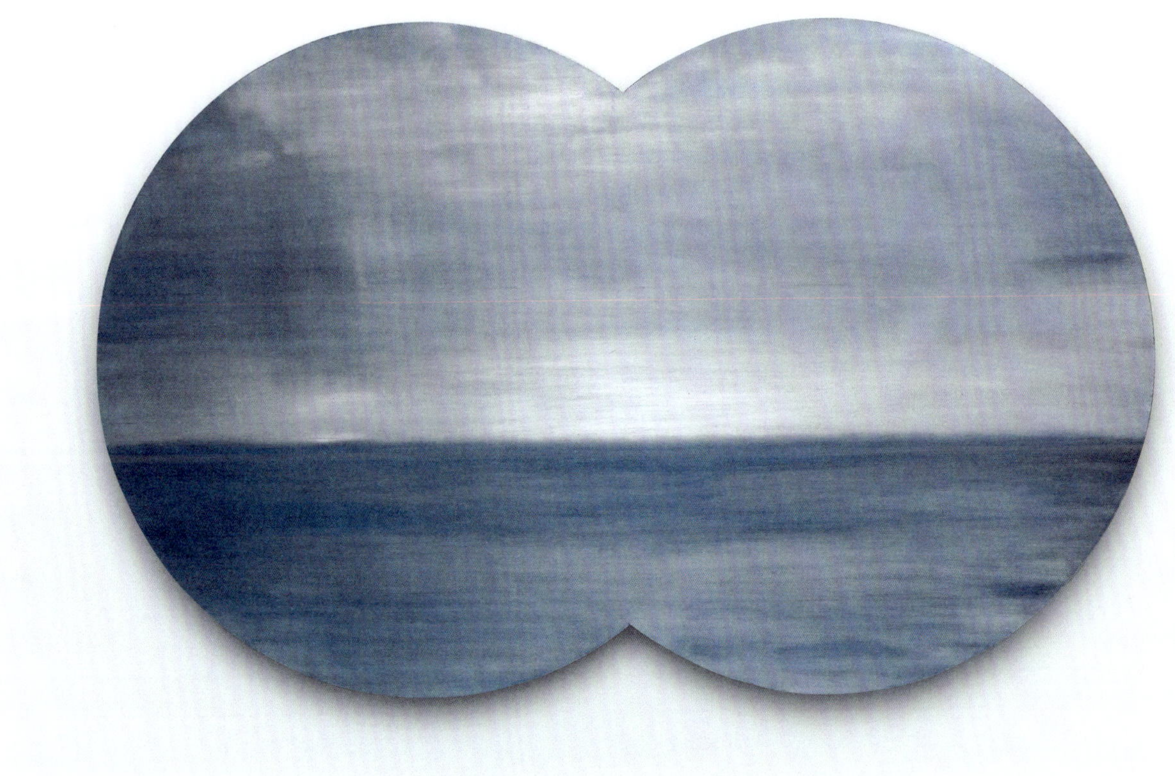

Dosen für Pulverkaffee, während Raetz für die grösseren Versionen Zinkblech verwendete. In vielen Fällen handelt es sich dabei um Klischeeplatten für Druckgrafiken, die er für die Reliefs in die gewünschte Form brachte.[7] Zwei entsprechend zugeschnittene Platten sah er auch für Radierungen vor; die eine verwendete er für die Kaltnadelarbeit *Sehfeld* von 1986 (Abb. 2)[8], aus der zweiten, grafisch unbearbeitet gebliebenen Platte entstand zehn Jahre später schliesslich der kleine *Zeemansblik* Nummer 16 (Abb. 3).[9] Im Februar 1987 kaufte Raetz zwei Platten Titanzink in den Massen 100×200 Zentimeter und in den Stärken 0,7 und 1 Millimeter.[10] Dieses vor allem für Fassaden, Dächer und Dachrinnen verwendete Material wählte er für die zwei grössten Fassungen von *Zeemansblik*. Beide befinden sich in Museumsbesitz.[11]

Das grösste Exemplar, die Nummer 11 der Werkreihe, wurde im Jahr 2000 vom Aargauer Kunsthaus in Aarau erworben. Es entstand im März 1987.[12] Aus diesem Jahr, datiert auf Anfang März, stammen auch die Fassungen Nummer

2
Sehfeld / Field of View, 1986
Kaltnadel, Polierstahl und Schmirgelpapier / Dry point, burnisher and sandpaper, 13×20,8 cm
Nachlass / Estate of Markus Raetz, Bern

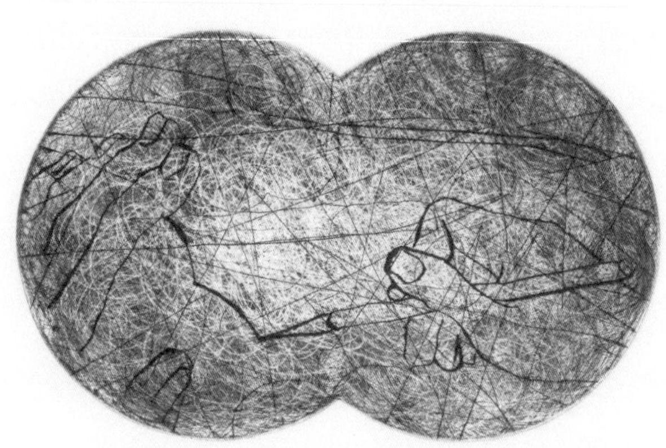

Swiss Pavilion at the Venice Biennale.[16] That same year, several versions could be seen together at the New Museum of Contemporary Art in New York, and likewise in 1989 at the Museum für Gegenwartskunst in Basel.

In tandem with its first exhibitions in 1986, *Zeemansblik* also made its appearance in publications. The magazine *Parkett*, which played an important role in fostering the international profile of contemporary artists, devoted its eighth volume primarily to Markus Raetz. Illustrations of *Zeemansblik* number 1 appear on the front cover and three full pages before the Content [sic] page, while the sections of an essay in German, and likewise those of its English translation, are separated by in total eight different views of the relief in the form of vignettes.[17] The Aarau *Zeemansblik* was even chosen to represent Swiss postwar art: it is reproduced on the front cover of *Rücksicht. 40 Jahre Kunst in der Schweiz*, a comprehensive overview of Swiss art since 1960, published in 2000 by the Aargauer Kunsthaus.[18] As shown by its continual inclusion in exhibitions over many decades, and by its equally regular reception in the art-historical literature and the visual arts, *Zeemansblik* is one of Markus Raetz's best-known and most popular works and has moreover itself become a motif of art. It is no coincidence that the collection of the Aargauer Kunsthaus houses works by Max Matter (b. 1941) and Michel Grillet (b. 1956) that cite the relief (figs. 4, 5). Gaspare O. Melcher (b. 1945) paid homage to Raetz with a paraphrase of *Zeemansblik*. (fig. 6).[19]

3
Zeemansblik, 1996
Zinkblech (Klischeeplatte), gefalzt /
Zinc sheet (cliché plate), folded,
13,1 × 21 × 0,9 cm
Nachlass / Estate of Markus Raetz, Bern

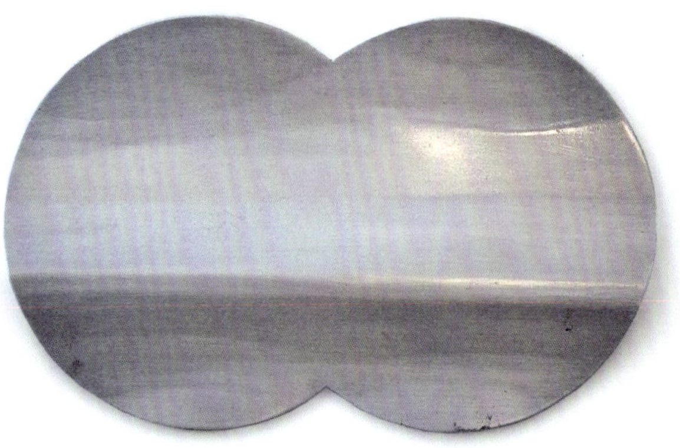

9 und 10. Rund die Hälfte der Gruppe, die Nummern 1 bis 8, war zwischen Juli 1985 und Juli 1986 entstanden, die Versionen 12 bis 15 stammen von 1988, und mit grösserer zeitlicher Unterbrechung folgten schliesslich die Exemplare 16 im Jahr 1996 und 17 sogar erst 1999.

Einige der Werke, die in seinem Œuvre eine entscheidende Rolle spielen, variierte Markus Raetz in mehreren Fassungen, zum Teil über einen grossen Zeitraum hinweg. Die stattliche Zahl der *Zeemansblik*-Versionen, die im Verlauf von knapp eineinhalb Jahrzehnten entstanden, ist daher ein starker Beleg für die Wichtigkeit dieses Werktypus. Im Unterschied zu anderen Hauptwerken fällt allerdings auf, dass sich die einzelnen Exemplare fast nur in der Grösse, und zwar beträchtlich, unterscheiden, während sie in Material und Form nur geringfügig voneinander abweichen.[13] Blech als Werkstoff und die charakteristische Form der gekuppelten Kreisscheiben standen schon mit der Nummer 1 ein für alle Mal fest und bedurften keiner weiteren Optimierung. Jede Variation hätte wohl eher eine Verunklärung als eine Erweiterung der Aussage zur Folge gehabt.[14] Selbst die späteren Bearbeitungen des Motivs in der Druckgrafik blieben der Erscheinung der Reliefs auffallend treu.[15] Am offensichtlichsten wird die Bedeutung von *Zeemansblik* in der Tatsache, dass das Relief – vor allem die grösseren Exemplare – seit 1986 in den allermeisten Ausstellungen, an denen Raetz mit umfangreichen Werkgruppen auftrat, präsent war. Am häufigsten zeigte er die grosse Aarauer Fassung; sie ist zwischen 1993 und 2023 in rund 20 Ausstellungen nachgewiesen.

4
Max Matter
Sehsea, 1995
Digitales Transferverfahren / Digital transfer process, 50×70 cm
Aargauer Kunsthaus, Aarau

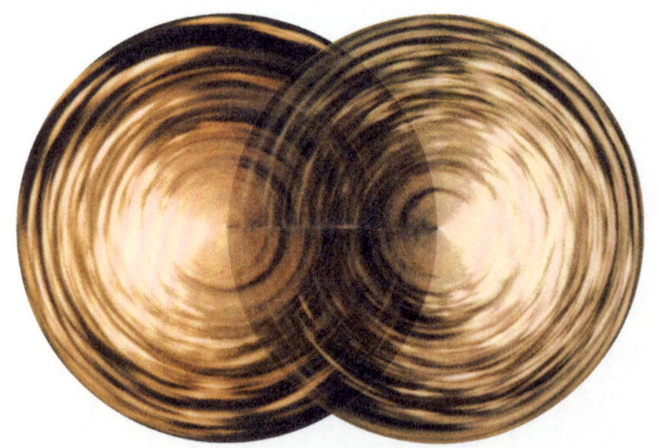

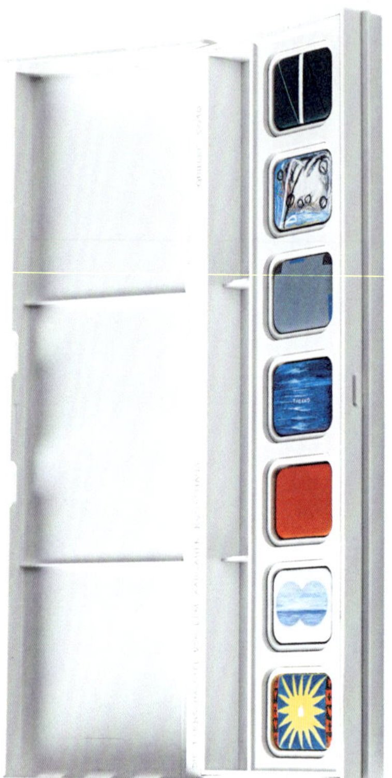

5
Michel Grillet
Die Farbschachtel von dem Aargauer Kunsthaus / The Color Box from the Aargauer Kunsthaus, 2010
Farbschachtel aus Plastik / Plastic paint box, 8,5×25,3×2,5 cm, Gouache auf Gouachepastillen / gouache on gouache pastilles, je / each 2,9×3,4 cm
Aargauer Kunsthaus, Aarau, Schenkung / Gift of Michel und / and Raffaella Grillet

The Title: The Importance of Language for the Work

The title *Zeemansblik* is a Dutch compound noun. It is made up of the determiner *zeeman*, which in English means seafarer or sailor, and the root word *blik*, meaning view, and can thus be translated literally as "sailor's view" and more freely as "sea view." The noun *blik* also has the second meaning of tin (as in metal) and tin (as in can). The title therefore explains the shape of the work: this shape is defined as a binocular field of view, and what can be seen within it as the view of the sea as it presents itself to a sailor. Furthermore, the title refers to the material from which the work is made. The dual meaning of *blik* thus interweaves statements about the work's shape, motif, and material properties.[20] Every translation of *Zeemansblik* into another language must either offer ungainly literal alternatives in order to do justice to the two meanings (in French, for example, *Vue/tôle du marin*, or *Vision ou tôle du marin*), or suppress one aspect and thereby ignore the ambiguity of Raetz's title. In these latter cases, the foreign-language title variant invariably confines itself to the motif of the view (*Seemannsblick, Mariner's Look, Seaman's Look, Sailor's Glance, Sailor's View, Merimiehen Näkymä*). The vocabulary employed in these translations is nevertheless helpful for the visual perception and linguistic reception of Raetz's work.

6
Gaspare Otto Melcher
Hommage an Raetz / Tribute to Raetz, 2013
Collage auf Leinwand / Collage on canvas, 95 x 95 cm
im Besitz des Künstlers / in possession of the artist

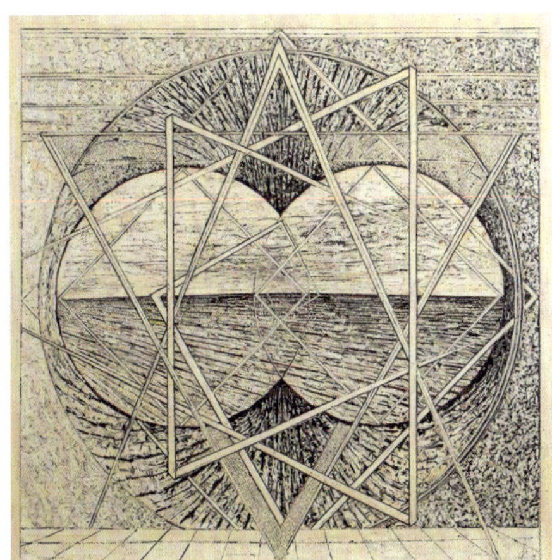

Bei vielen handelte es sich um repräsentative Überblicke über sein Schaffen, in denen die Anwesenheit von *Zeemansblik* unabdingbar war, oder der Ausstellungsort besass wegen seines Renommees eine besondere Ausstrahlungskraft wie beispielsweise 1988 der Schweizer Pavillon an der Biennale von Venedig.[16] Im selben Jahr waren im New Museum of Contemporary Art in New York sogar mehrere Fassungen zu sehen, desgleichen 1989 im Museum für Gegenwartskunst in Basel.

Zeitgleich mit den ersten Ausstellungen im Jahr 1986 war *Zeemansblik* auch in Publikationen präsent. In der für die internationale Wahrnehmung eines Künstlers relevanten Zeitschrift *Parkett*, die ihre achte Ausgabe in erster Linie Markus Raetz widmete, zieren Abbildungen der Nummer 1 der Werkgruppe den Umschlag sowie drei ganze Seiten vor dem Inhaltsverzeichnis, acht verschiedene Ansichten trennen als Vignetten die Abschnitte eines Textes und seiner englischen Fassung.[17] Dem Aarauer *Zeemansblik* wurde sogar die Ehre zuteil, die Schweizer Nachkriegskunst zu repräsentieren. Er ist auf dem Umschlag der im Jahr 2000 vom Aargauer Kunsthaus herausgegebenen umfangreichen Publikation *Rücksicht. 40 Jahre Kunst in der Schweiz* abgebildet.[18] Die über Jahrzehnte selbstverständliche Anwesenheit in Ausstellungen und die ebenso kontinuierliche schriftliche und bildliche Rezeption weisen *Zeemansblik* als eines der bekanntesten und populärsten Werke von Markus Raetz aus, das im Übrigen selbst zum Motiv von Kunstwerken wurde. Wohl nicht zufällig befinden sich gerade in der Sammlung des Aargauer Kunsthauses Arbeiten von Max Matter (*1941) und Michel Grillet (*1956), die das Relief zitieren (Abb. 4, 5). Gaspare O. Melcher (*1945) widmete Raetz eine Hommage mit der Paraphrase von *Zeemansblik* (Abb. 6).[19]

Der Titel: die Bedeutung der Sprache für das Werk

Der Titel *Zeemansblik* ist ein niederländisches Nominalkompositum, das aus dem Bestimmungswort *zeeman* für Seemann oder Matrose und dem Grundwort *blik* für Blick besteht und wörtlich mit «Blick des Matrosen» und freier mit «Meeresblick» oder «Seeblick» zu übersetzen ist. Das Substantiv *blik* hat zudem die Bedeutung von Blech, Dose und Büchse. Der Titel erklärt somit die Form des Werks. Sie wird als binokulares Gesichtsfeld definiert und das darin Sichtbare als der Anblick des Meeres, wie er sich einem Seemann darbietet. Darüber hinaus verweist der Titel auf das Material, aus dem das Werk besteht. Die Mehrdeutigkeit

Within Raetz's sculptural œuvre we find titles in no fewer than eight different languages: Dutch, English, French, German, Italian, Korean, Spanish, and Swiss German. Homonyms regularly play a role, as for example in Raetz's series of large drawings of faces, in which a magnolia leaf takes the place of the mouth: in Korean, *ib* (mouth) sounds almost the same as the word *ip* (foliage).[21] The Dutch *Zeemansblik* thus lent itself as a title for semantic reasons. But it has a biographical connection, too. From 1969 to 1973, Markus Raetz and his partner Monika lived in Amsterdam and were familiar with the Dutch language, which the artist employed in a number of his work titles. Raetz's delight in wordplay in several languages runs through his entire œuvre, including his drawings. Raetz thereby revealed a particular preference for equivocation in all its variations, which he explored in numerous lists of homographic and homophonic words and with so-called false friends in other languages. He was also interested in anagrams and palindromes. All of this found its way into the titles of his works.[22] From the beginning, too, letters and words made up an important part of the iconography of his drawings and sculptures—an aspect of his œuvre that in 2022 formed the subject of a dedicated exhibition and a publication.[23]

Many work titles are more than mere aids to identification and differentiation. They serve less as descriptions than as instructions on how to view the work. Indeed, work and title are often complementary or mutually dependent. The title determines our perception of the work, and the visual evidence of the work sheds light on the linguistic idiosyncrasy of the title. Language assumes a semantic significance in a broader sense, too. This is the case, for example, with Raetz's installation *Chambre de lecture* (fig. 7). Here, the title associates the profiles of human faces, suspended in rows along the walls of a room, where they gently rotate, with books in a library or with the words of a text, and equates looking at them with reading this text.[24] When asked about his profile drawings in an interview in 2014, Raetz responded: "With drawing, you can do something similar as with writing, namely describe a character. For me, the profiles are almost like letters."[25] He based the layout of his large hedge maze *Le Palindrome* of 2011–2016 on a Latin palindrome.[26] The forks in the maze correspond to the sequence of letters in the palindrome: depending on whether the letter in question is a vowel or a consonant, visitors must turn right or left in order to take the direct route to the center and back to the exit.

von *blik* verschränkt somit Aussagen zur Form, zum Motiv und zur materiellen Beschaffenheit.[20] Jede Übersetzung von *Zeemansblik* in eine andere Sprache führt zwangsläufig zu unschönen Verdoppelungen, um den beiden Bedeutungen gerecht zu werden (*Vue/tôle du marin, Vision ou tôle du marin*), oder unterdrückt einen inhaltlichen Aspekt und unterschlägt die Ambivalenz von Raetz' Werktitel. In diesen Fällen beschränkt sich die fremdsprachige Titelvariante immer auf das Motiv des Blicks (*Seemannsblick, Mariner's Look, Seaman's Look, Sailor's Glance, Sailor's View, Merimiehen Näkymä*). Immerhin liefern die Übersetzungen ein kleines Vokabular der visuellen Wahrnehmung, das für die Betrachtung und sprachliche Rezeption von Raetz' Werk hilfreich ist.

Für Raetz' skulpturales Œuvre sind Titel in acht Sprachen dokumentiert (Deutsch, Englisch, Französisch, Italienisch, Koreanisch, Niederländisch, Schweizerdeutsch, Spanisch). Homonyme Begriffe spielen wiederholt eine Rolle, etwa bei der Serie von grossen Gesichtszeichnungen, bei denen ein Magnolienblatt an die Stelle des Mundes gesetzt ist: *ib* bedeutet auf Koreanisch Mund und klingt fast gleich wie das Wort *ip* für ein Laubblatt.[21] Das niederländische *Zeemansblik* bot sich also aus semantischen Gründen als Titel an. Es gibt aber auch einen biografischen Bezug. Markus Raetz und seine Partnerin Monika lebten von 1969 bis 1973 in Amsterdam und waren mit der niederländischen Sprache vertraut; sie kam in etlichen Werktiteln zur Anwendung. Die Freude an Wortspielen in mehreren Sprachen durchzieht Raetz' gesamtes Werk, auch das zeichnerische. Dabei zeigt sich eine Vorliebe für alle Varianten der Äquivokation, die er in zahlreichen Listen aus homographen und homophonen Wörtern oder – sprachenübergreifend – mit sogenannten falschen Freunden durchspielte. Anagramme und Palindrome interessierten ihn ebenso. All das schlug sich in einigen Werktiteln nieder.[22] Zudem machten Buchstaben und Wörter von Beginn an in seinem zeichnerischen wie skulpturalen Werk einen bedeutenden Teil der Ikonografie aus. Diesem Aspekt seines Schaffens waren 2022 sogar eine Ausstellung und eine Publikation gewidmet.[23]

Viele Werktitel sind mehr als blosse Hilfsmittel zur Identifikation und Unterscheidung. Sie dienen weniger der Beschreibung als der Betrachtungsanweisung, ja oftmals ergänzen sich Werk und Titel oder hängen voneinander ab: Der Titel bestimmt unsere Wahrnehmung des Werks, und dessen visuelle Evidenz erhellt die sprachliche Eigenheit des Titels. Der Sprache kommt auch in

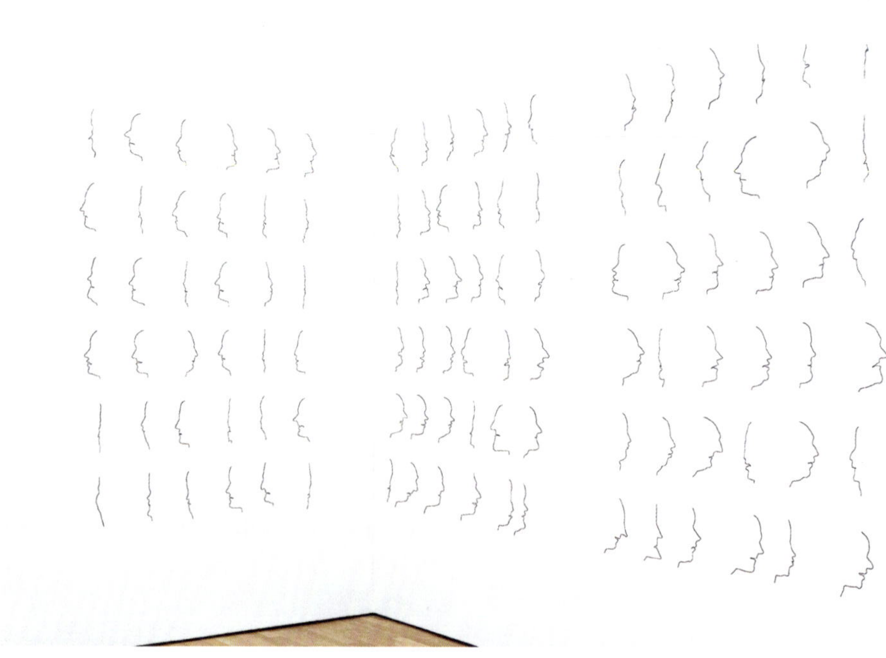

The way in which visitors experience the interior of the labyrinth thus literally follows a text.

Raetz was a passionate reader all his life and his works contain many quotations and even more allusions to literary motifs from a wide range of sources. He therefore titled a face he "discovered" in the grain of a block of wood with *Saint Possible*, a name from the *Calendrier pataphysique*.[27] He took the title of a relief from a story by science-fiction author Isaac Asimov (1920–1992),[28] while the name *MIMI* for his sculptural stick figures has a source in the French novel *Boomerang* by Michel Butor (1926–2016), where it is associated with almost disembodied nature spirits in Australian aboriginal mythology.[29] The anamorphic word sculpture *ME – WE* is a reference to the eponymous mini-poem by the African-American heavyweight boxer and civil rights activist Muhammad Ali (born Cassius Clay, 1942–2016).[30] In a print of the same subject, which he titled *ME – WE (Dix. Muhammad Ali)*, Raetz made this authorship clear.[31] The catoptric (mirror) anamorphosis revealing the name *ALICE* takes up motifs from *Through the Looking-Glass* by Lewis Carroll (1832–1898), the sequel to *Alice's Adventures in Wonderland* (fig. 8).[32] While it is true that the objects making up the work group *Freedom and Beauty* cite visual sources, these latter are illustrations accompanying the art-theoretical treatise *The Analysis of Beauty. Written with a View of Fixing the Fluctuating Ideas of Taste* by William Hogarth (1697–1764) and the novel *The Life and Opinions of Tristram Shandy,*

7
Chambre de lecture / Reading Room, 2013–2015
432 Plastiken: Eisendraht, Aufhängung: Polyamidfaden / 432 sculptures: steel wire, suspended on polyamide thread, 400×815×630 cm (Masse des Raums der Erstpräsentation / dimensions of the room in which the installation was presented for the first time, Museo d'arte della Svizzera italiana, Lugano 2016. Die Abb. zeigt einen Ausschnitt der Präsentation in Lugano / The figure shows a detail from the Lugano presentation)
Privatbesitz / Private collection

einem umfassenderen Verständnis sinnstiftende Bedeutung zu. Das ist beispielsweise bei der *Chambre de lecture* genannten Rauminstallation der Fall (Abb. 7). Hier assoziiert der Titel die Gesichtsprofile, die entlang der Wände eines Raums aufgereiht sind und sich bewegen, mit Büchern in einer Bibliothek oder mit Wörtern eines Textes und setzt ihre Betrachtung dem Lesen dieses Textes gleich.[24] Auf seine gezeichneten Profile angesprochen, erklärte Raetz 2014 in einem Interview: «Mit Zeichnen kann man etwas Ähnliches machen wie mit Schrift, nämlich einen Charakter beschreiben. Die Profile sind für mich fast wie Buchstaben.»[25] Der Wegführung seines grossen Heckenlabyrinths *Le Palindrome* (2011–2016) legte er ein lateinisches Satzpalindrom zugrunde.[26] Die Verzweigungen entsprechen der Buchstabenfolge des Palindroms, und der direkte Weg ins Zentrum und wieder zurück zum Ausgang ist, je nachdem, ob es sich um einen Vokal oder einen Konsonanten handelt, nach rechts oder links einzuschlagen. Die Raumerfahrung der Besucherinnen und Besucher des Labyrinths vollzieht sich also buchstäblich nach dem Muster eines Textes.

Raetz war zeitlebens ein leidenschaftlicher Leser, und in seinen Werken gibt es etliche Zitate und noch mehr Anspielungen auf literarische Motive unterschiedlichster Herkunft. So betitelte er ein in der Maserung eines Balkens entdecktes Gesicht mit *Saint Possible*, einem Namen aus dem *Calendrier pataphysique*.[27] Für ein Relief übernahm er den Titel einer Erzählung des Science-Fiction-Autors Isaac Asimov (1920–1992)[28] und der Name «MIMI» für seine skulpturalen Strichfiguren hat eine Quelle in Michel Butors (1926–2016) Roman *Boomerang*, wo er mit fast körperlosen Naturwesen in der Mythologie der australischen Aborigines verbunden ist.[29] Die anamorphotische Wortplastik *ME – WE* ist eine Reverenz an das gleichlautende Kürzestgedicht des afroamerikanischen Schwergewichtsboxers und Bürgerrechtlers Muhammad Ali (alias Cassius Clay, 1942–2016).[30] Der Titelzusatz *Dix. Muhammad Ali* für eine Druckgrafik mit einem vergleichbaren Sujet legt diese Autorschaft offen.[31] Die katoptrische Wortanamorphose *ALICE* greift Motive aus Lewis Carrolls (1832–1898) Erzählung *Alice hinter den Spiegeln* auf, der Fortsetzung von *Alice im Wunderland* (Abb. 8).[32] Die Fassungen der Gruppe *Freedom and Beauty* zitieren zwar grafische Vorbilder, diese haben aber in William Hogarths (1697–1764) Traktat *The Analysis of Beauty. Written with a View of Fixing the Fluctuating Ideas of Taste* einen kunsttheoretischen und mit dem Roman *The Life and Opinions of Tristram Shandy, Gentleman*

8
ALICE, 2004/2008
Ex. / No. 6/6
Messingguss, patiniert / Cast brass, patinated, 40×5,3×24,5 cm,
beschichtete Glasscheibe / coated glass pane, 62×49×0,6 cm,
Plinthe: Eichenholz, gebeizt und gewachst / plinth: oak, stained and waxed, 2,5×62×31 cm,
Sockel: Holz / base: wood, 116×63×32 cm
Nachlass / Estate of Markus Raetz, Bern

Gentleman by Laurence Sterne (1713–1768), and so have a literary background.[33] In 1980 Raetz designed a series of fourteen prints for the German edition of the fantastical book *Impressions d'Afrique* by Raymond Roussel (1877–1933).[34] In 1978 he used a portrait of the poet Robert Walser (1878–1956), whom he greatly admired, as the motif for a relief, and some eleven years later paid homage to him in the form of a sculptural stele in front of the Neues Museum in Biel.[35]

Raetz's interest in the interaction between language and the work of visual art, and especially in the intricate relationship between an object, its representation, and its name, links him with probably his two most important artistic points of reference: Marcel Duchamp (1887–1968) and René Magritte (1898–1967). Raetz adopted work titles from both, and on other occasions subtly commented on their titles in his own. *Why Not Sneeze, Rose Sélavy?*, the deliberately nonsensical title that Duchamp gave to a semi-readymade of 1921,[36] is adapted by Raetz to become *Warum nicht Niesen*. Raetz's title plays on the German verb *niesen*, to sneeze, and so takes up Duchamp's "Why not sneeze?" (figs. 9, 10). But Niesen is also the name of a Swiss mountain, and consequently the question "Why not [Mount] Niesen?" contributes to our understanding of the work and at the same time only makes sense in front of it.[37] From Magritte Raetz took up the title *La seconde nature*,[38] and in his anamorphic sculpture *Nichtpfeife*[39] paraphrased Magritte's famous painting *The Treachery of Images*, with its matter-of-fact representation of a tobacco pipe and, written underneath in neat school script, the assertion "Ceci n'est pas une pipe" (figs. 11, 12).[40] In 1991 he manipulated a reproduction of this painting in a series of photocopies.[41] Raetz expressly referred to his engagement with Magritte in the context of his word sculptures, too: "I'm constantly thinking about how René Magritte uses words."[42] He was primarily alluding not to Magritte's at times enigmatic work titles, but to the way he incorporated words into his paintings. With regards to the word *Zeemansblik*, the importance that Raetz attached to it can be seen in the fact that he coined it not only for one group of works, but also used it in 1989, at his solo show at the Museum für Gegenwartskunst in Basel, for an entire room containing several reliefs from the series.[43]

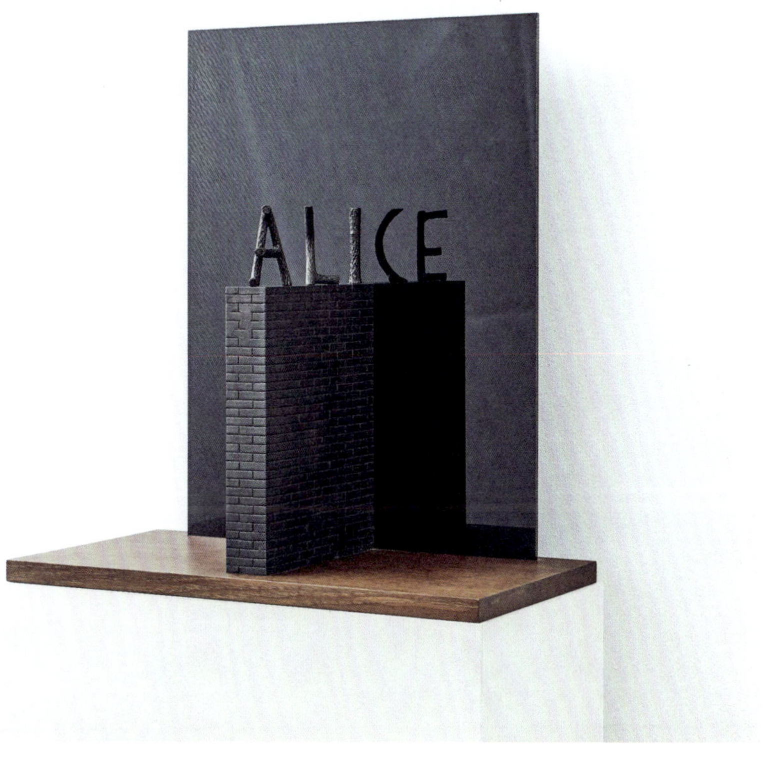

von Laurence Sterne (1713–1768) einen literarischen Hintergrund.[33] 1980 gestaltete Raetz eine Folge von 14 Druckgrafiken für die deutsche Ausgabe des fantastischen Buches *Impressions d'Afrique* von Raymond Roussel (1877–1933).[34] Ein Bildnis des von ihm sehr geschätzten Dichters Robert Walser (1878–1956) verwendete er 1978 als Motiv eines Reliefs, ein gutes Jahrzehnt später widmete er ihm eine Hommage in Form einer Bildstele vor dem Neuen Museum in Biel.[35]

Raetz' Beschäftigung mit der Wechselwirkung zwischen Sprache und bildkünstlerischem Werk und besonders mit dem vertrackten Verhältnis zwischen einem Gegenstand, seiner Darstellung und seiner Benennung verbindet ihn mit seinen zwei wohl wichtigsten künstlerischen Bezugsgrössen Marcel Duchamp (1887–1968) und René Magritte (1898–1967). Von beiden übernahm er Werktitel oder kommentierte sie hintersinnig mit seinen eigenen Arbeiten. Duchamps gezielt sinnlose Bezeichnung *Why Not Sneeze, Rose Sélavy?* für ein Semi-Readymade von 1921[36] lautet in Raetz' Adaption *Warum nicht Niesen* (Abb. 9, 10). Bei ihm trägt die Frage zum Verständnis des Werks bei, das seinerseits der Frage überhaupt erst Sinn verleiht.[37] Von Magritte griff er den Titel *La seconde nature*[38] auf und paraphrasierte mit seiner anamorphotischen Skulptur *Nichtpfeife*[39] des-

9
Warum nicht Niesen / Why Not Sneeze or *Why Not Mount Niesen*, 1978/2005
Rahmen aus Holz, Glasscheibe, Kupferdraht, Stahlnagel / Wood frame, glass, copper wire, steel nail, 60 x 77,5 x 2,2 cm
Privatbesitz / Private collection

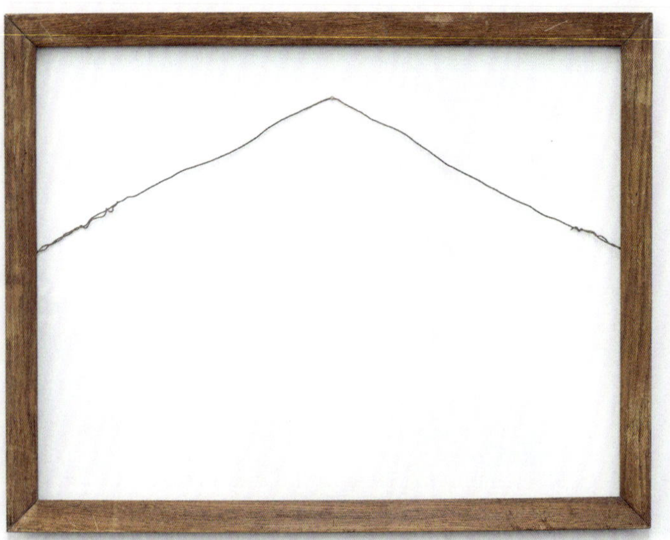

10
Marcel Duchamp
Why Not Sneeze, Rose Sélavy? / Warum nicht niesen, Rose Sélavy?, 1921
152 Marmorkuben, Thermometer, Sepiaschale in einem Vogelkäfig /
152 marble cubes, thermometer, cuttlebone in a birdcage, 11,4 x 22 x 16 cm
Philadelphia Museum of Art, The Louise and Walter Arensberg Collection

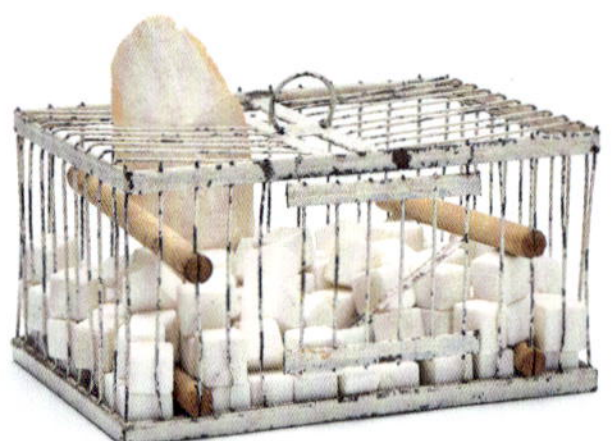

The Genesis of *Zeemansblik*: A Short Upbeat and a Long Prehistory

A text reporting in a factual style is only partially able to convey the genesis of a work by Markus Raetz. The additive sequence of statements inevitably corresponds to a line, be it straight or meandering. In the evolution of Raetz's œuvre, however, one thing does not simply lead to the next, and this in turn to another. His artistic development must instead be pictured in terms of a highly complex, irregular, and three-dimensional network, one that is almost impossible to map out in a comprehensible form in words. Within this network, each work represents a node that is connected to numerous others. The connections between these nodes can be simple and easy to follow, or they can be convoluted and span lengthy periods of time. At the heart of Raetz's concept of the artwork, moreover, lies not the individual artefact but the entire creative process: whether a rapid sketch, a painting, a study for a sculpture or the staging of an entire exhibition, everything possesses fundamentally the same value. Hence any account of the genesis of a single work necessarily remains patchy, and each comparative example, although not arbitrary, is just one possibility among many others. In the catalog of Raetz's first major retrospective in 1986, Toni Stooss chose a different image to describe the way in which retrospection and

11
René Magritte
La trahision des images /
The Treachery of Images, 1929
Öl auf Leinwand / Oil on canvas,
60 x 81 cm
Los Angeles County Museum of Art,
Los Angeles

12
Nichtpfeife / Non-pipe, 1990/1992
Ex. / No. 1/6
Eisenguss, partiell patiniert / Cast iron, partly patinated,
26 x 55 x 33 cm
Privatbesitz / Private collection

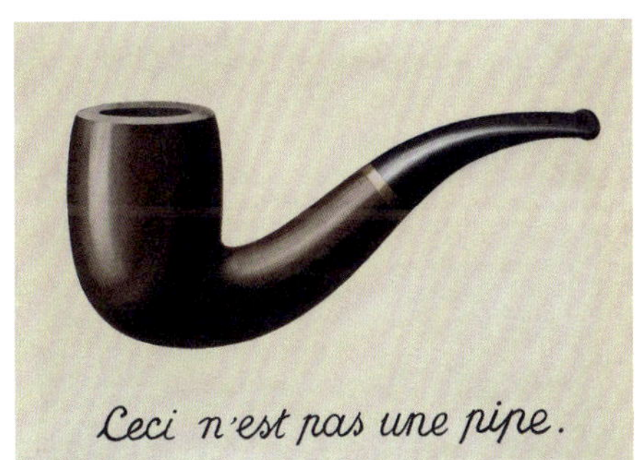

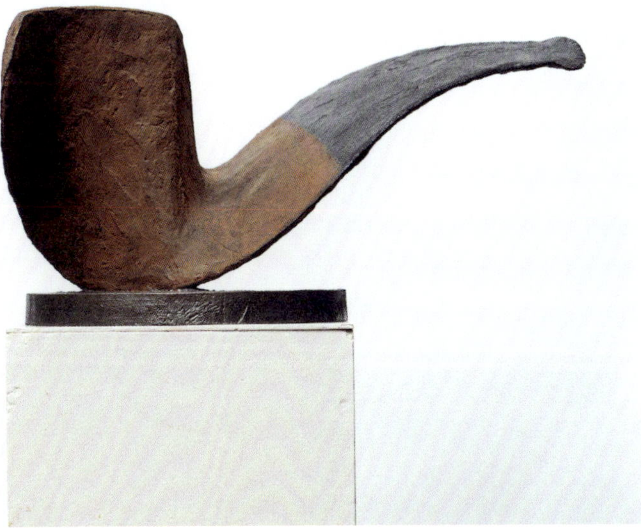

sen berühmtes Bild *La trahison des images* mit der sachlichen Wiedergabe einer Tabakpfeife und der in fein säuberlicher Schulschrift daruntergesetzten Behauptung «Ceci n'est pas une pipe» (Abb. 11, 12).[40] Eine Reproduktion dieses Bildes verfremdete er 1991 in einer Reihe von Fotokopien.[41] Auf seine Auseinandersetzung mit Magritte verwies Raetz ausdrücklich auch im Zusammenhang mit seinen Wortplastiken: «Ich denke immer wieder darüber nach, wie René Magritte die Wörter braucht.»[42] Er sprach damit nicht in erster Linie Magrittes teils enigmatische Werktitel an, sondern die Art, wie dieser Wörter in seinen Gemälden ins Bild setzte. Was das Wort *Zeemansblik* betrifft, so zeigt sich die Wichtigkeit, die Raetz ihm beimass, auch im Umstand, dass er es nicht nur für einen Werktypus prägte, sondern es 1989 im Basler Museum für Gegenwartskunst für einen ganzen Ausstellungsraum mit mehreren Reliefs der Serie verwendete.[43]

Die Genese von *Zeemansblik*: kurzer Auftakt und lange Vorgeschichte

Das Medium des sachlich rapportierenden Textes ist nur bedingt geeignet, die Genese eines Werks von Markus Raetz zu vermitteln. Die additive Reihung von Aussagen entspricht gezwungenermassen einer Linie, sei sie gerade oder mäandrierend. In Raetz' Werkentwicklung führt aber nicht einfach eines zum Nächsten

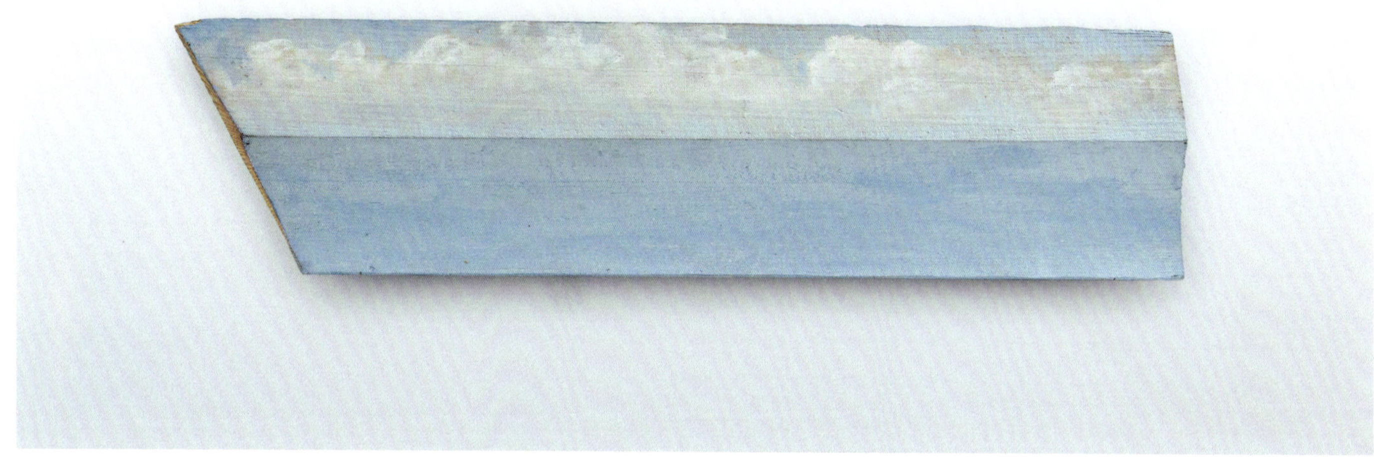

progress are intertwined in Raetz's work. He spoke of a conically widening spiral, whose coils are connected by lines that start from the tip of the cone as the beginning of the artist's career. "Applied to Markus Raetz's œuvre, these lines would connect 'themes' of various kinds, such as the use of a certain technique, a reprised structure, a recurring visual motif, or even the same basic idea, in each case formulated in different sensory terms."[44] This image has the advantage that it invokes a figure—the three-dimensional spiral—used by Raetz himself to explain his way of working as a continual process of returning to and reprising his earlier work in productive ways. The spiral runs through his entire œuvre, and in particular his sculptural work from the 1990s onwards, as a highly variable leitmotif. As Gilbert Lascault declared in as early as 1986: "M. R. loves spirals. Above all else."[45]

The immediate precursors to *Zeemansblik* were produced in two phases in quick succession, and already exhibit the key aspects of the marine motif and the execution as a relief. The first, dating from January 1985, is a processed found object, namely a length of wooden molding which the artist has painted in a light blue and whose profile corresponds almost exactly to the sculptural form of *Zeemansblik* (fig. 13).[46] To reinforce the association with the sea-and-sky motif, the upper half of the molding is painted with naturalistic banks of billowing cloud. In variants made at this same point in time using light blue paper, Raetz even dispensed entirely with painterly interventions. A single

13
Ohne Titel / Untitled, 1985/1989
Ölfarbe auf Holzleiste /
Oil on wooden molding,
1,6×48,3×2,8 cm
Nachlass / Estate of Markus Raetz, Bern

und dieses wieder zu einem Weiteren. Statt von einer Linie der künstlerischen Entwicklung müsste man eher von einer höchst komplexen, unregelmässigen und dreidimensionalen Netzstruktur ausgehen, die sprachlich kaum in verständlicher Form abzubilden wäre. Jedes Werk stellt einen Knoten in diesem Netz dar, der mit zahlreichen anderen verbunden ist. Die Verbindungen zwischen diesen Knoten können einfach und leicht nachvollziehbar sein oder selbst verwickelt und grössere Zeiträume überbrückend. Im Mittelpunkt von Raetz' Werkbegriff stand zudem nicht das einzelne Artefakt, sondern der gesamte kreative Prozess, in dem alles Geschaffene prinzipiell den gleichen Wert besitzt, unabhängig davon, ob es sich um eine flüchtige Skizze, ein Bild, eine plastische Studie oder eine ganze Ausstellungsinszenierung handelt. Die Beschreibung der Genese eines singulären Werks bleibt daher notwendigerweise lückenhaft, und jedes Vergleichsbeispiel ist, wenn auch nicht beliebig, so doch nur eine Möglichkeit unter vielen anderen. Toni Stooss wählte im Katalog von Raetz' erster grosser Retrospektive 1986 ein anderes Bild, um die Art der Verschränkung von Rückblick und Fortschritt in seinem Schaffen zu umschreiben. Er sprach von einer kegelförmig sich weitenden Spirale, deren Windungen durch Linien verbunden sind, die von der Kegelspitze als dem Beginn seines Schaffens ausgehen: «Auf das Werk von Markus Raetz übertragen wären durch jene Linien ‹Themen› verschiedener Qualität verbunden: etwa die Anwendung einer bestimmten Technik, einer wieder aufgenommenen Struktur, eines wiederkehrenden Bildmotivs oder gar desselben Grundgedankens, der eine jeweils unterschiedliche sinnliche Formulierung erfährt.»[44] Diese Darstellung hat den Vorzug, dass sie mit der räumlichen Spirale eine Figur ins Spiel bringt, die Raetz selbst benutzte, um seine Arbeit als einen Prozess permanenter produktiver Rückgriffe zu erklären. Als höchst variables Leitmotiv durchzieht die Spirale sein gesamtes Schaffen, in besonderem Mass aber sein skulpturales Werk ab den 1990er Jahren. «M. R. liebt Spiralen. Über alles», stellte Gilbert Lascault schon in den 1980er Jahren fest.[45]

Die unmittelbaren Vorstufen von *Zeemansblik*, die schon die entscheidenden Aspekte des marinen Motivs und der Ausführung als Relief aufweisen, entstanden in zwei kurz aufeinanderfolgenden Phasen. Aus dem Januar 1985 stammt ein bearbeitetes Fundstück, eine hellblau gefasste hölzerne Leiste, deren Profil fast exakt der plastischen Form von *Zeemansblik* entspricht (Abb. 13).[46] Zur Unterstützung der motivischen Assoziation ist die obere Leistenkehle mit einem

14
Ohne Titel / Untitled, 1964
Dispersion auf ungrundierter Leinwand über Holzkonstruktion auf Sperrholzplatten, 2-teilig / Emulsion on unprimed canvas over wooden construction on plywood, 2-part, 30,2×44,4×8 cm,
Rahmen: Holz, bemalt / frame: wood, painted, 32×46,2×8 cm
Nachlass / Estate of Markus Raetz, Bern

horizontal fold divides the sheet across the center into sky and sea. In one example, the fold is complemented on the left-hand edge by creases, so that when seen in raking light the impression is created of rocky cliffs.[47] In July 1985, Raetz decided in favor of sheet metal. Before finally arriving at the binocular silhouette, he designed variants in the picture-like shape of a rectangle and as a tondo, which latter makes the relief appear as a view of the sea from a porthole.[48] The first version of *Zeemansblik* was finally created at the end of the same month.

The work has a much longer and more multifaceted prehistory, however. As far as its sculptural form is concerned, this prehistory can be traced back to the early 1960s. Toni Stooss condensed it into the formula "Vom Leinwandknick zum *Zeemansblik*" ("from canvas crease to *Zeemansblik*").[49] With the term "Leinwandknick," he was referring to reliefs dating from 1964. These consist of canvases, painted white or black, which are mounted on stretchers like traditional paintings. Wooden battens behind the canvas cause a crease in the surface, similar to the fold on the metal reliefs created two decades later. Two versions even anticipate the basic form of the coupled discs divided in linear fashion, even if they remain integrated within the conventional rectangular pictorial format (fig. 14).[50] At the same time, the double-circle figure played a renewed role in monochrome reliefs resembling paintings, whose three-dimen-

15
Ohne Titel / Untitled, 1964
Gumminoppenmatte, verformt und bemalt (Kunstharzspray «Duco-Spray»), Rahmen: Holz, bemalt / Rubber finger-brush mats, deformed and painted (synthetic resin "Duco Spray"), frame: wood, painted, 22,8 × 28,5 × 3,5 cm
Privatbesitz / Private collection

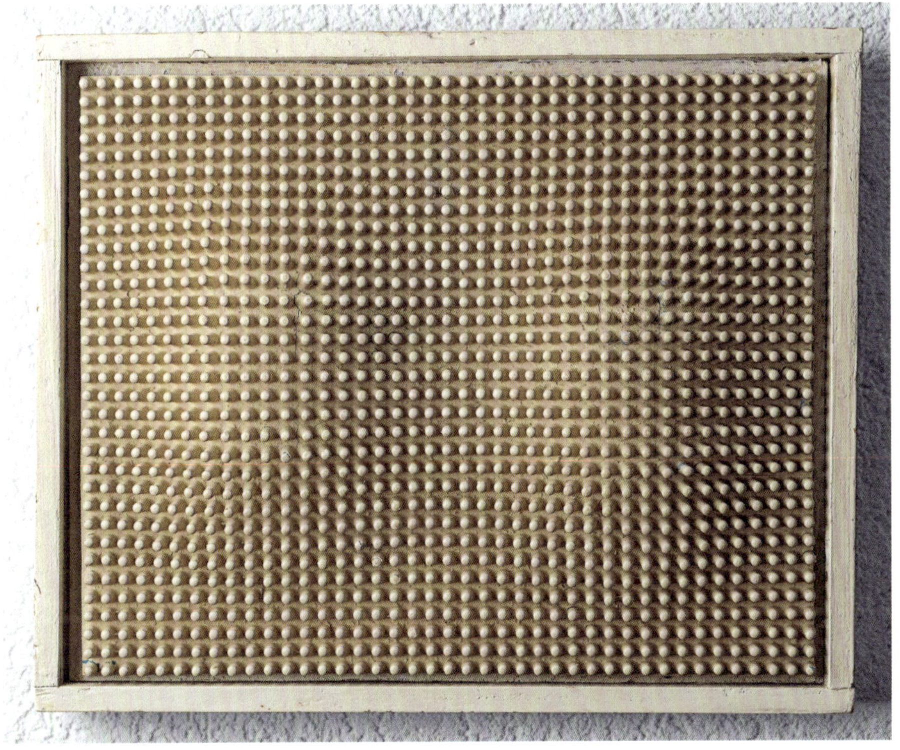

naturalistischen Wolkenhimmel bemalt. Bei gleichzeitigen Varianten aus hellblauem Papier verzichtete Raetz sogar ganz auf malerische Eingriffe. Ein einziger waagrechter Falz teilt das Blatt in der Mitte in Himmel und Meer. In einem Beispiel wird der Falz am linken Rand ergänzt durch Knitterfalten, so dass im Streiflicht der Eindruck einer felsigen Steilküste entsteht.[47] Im Juli 1985 entschied sich Raetz für den Werkstoff Blech. Bevor die binokulare Silhouette feststand, gestaltete er Varianten in der bildartigen Rechteckform und als Tondo, welches das Relief als Blick aus einem Bullauge auf das Meer erscheinen lässt.[48] Am Ende desselben Monats entstand schliesslich die erste Fassung von *Zeemansblik*.

Das Werk hat aber eine wesentlich längere und facettenreichere Vorgeschichte. Was seine plastische Form betrifft, reicht sie zurück bis in die frühen 1960er Jahre. Toni Stooss verknappte sie zur Formel «Vom Leinwandknick zum *Zeemansblik*».[49] Mit dem Begriff «Leinwandknick» bezog er sich auf Reliefs aus dem Jahr 1964. Es handelt sich um weiss oder schwarz bemalte Leinwände, die wie traditionelle Gemälde auf Chassis gespannt sind. Hinterlegte Leisten verformen die Oberfläche ähnlich wie der Falz die zwei Jahrzehnte jüngeren Blechreliefs. Zwei Versionen nehmen gar die Grundform der gekuppelten, linear unterteilten Scheiben vorweg, auch wenn sie noch in das konventionelle Bildrechteck integriert blieben (Abb. 14).[50] Die Doppelkreisfigur spielte zur gleichen Zeit erneut eine Rolle in wiederum monochromen, gemäldeartigen Reliefs, deren Plasti-

16
Zone blanche / White Zone, 1965
Dispersion auf Leinwand über Schaumstoff auf Holzfaserplatten, mehrteilig / Emulsion on canvas over foam on fiberboard, multipart, je / each ca. 255 cm (Höhe / height) zerstört / destroyed

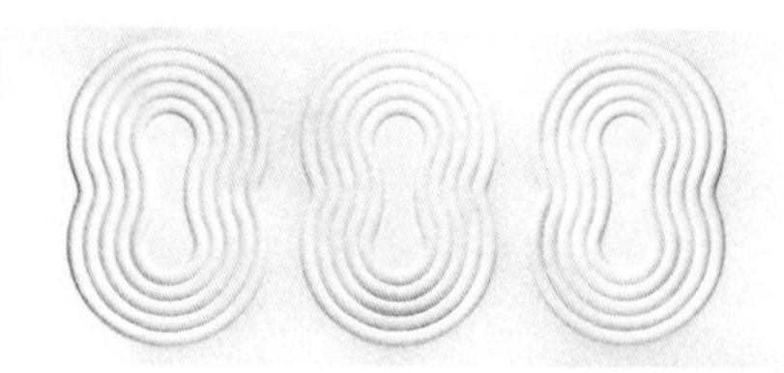

sionality derives from foam padding beneath the canvas. Common to both types of work is their hybrid mediality: the overall form and the canvas correspond to the traditional painting, but the protruding volumes, and the renunciation of the use of chromatic colors, belong to the realm of sculpture. This position in between media and the oscillation between two- and three-dimensional appearance were to characterize the whole of Markus Raetz's œuvre and become constitutive for *Zeemansblik*, too. Framed reliefs from this same point in time, consisting of rubber finger-brush mats exhibiting two adjacent spherical bulges, also belong in this context (fig. 15). They look ahead to *Zeemansblik* not only in their formal structure, but also in the industrial character of their rubber mats, which links them with the titanium zinc usually employed in construction and equally foreign to art.

The double-circle form underwent a first change in the padded canvas reliefs mentioned above. Its two circles are here aligned vertically and, in some cases, joined by a third. The figure as a whole is elongated, exhibits a harmoniously undulating contour, and may resemble a peanut[51] or a female torso. This transition to a defined figure served to liberate the non-representational form from the pictorial plane. The process whereby an originally two-dimensional graphic figure arrived at sculptural autonomy is exemplified in the case of Raetz's 1965 *Zone blanche*, the largest in a series of monochrome padded reliefs. At a later date, Raetz removed its central field and transformed it, with just a few painted lines, into the torso of a female nude (figs. 16, 17).[52] As well as assigning various aspects relating to content to one form, in other words, he was also able to translate an iconography that interested him into different materials. Around the time he defined the large canvas fragment as a torso, Raetz produced a tiny stone sculpture with the same motif in identical form (fig. 18). Like a sculpture in the round, however, its back has also been worked. Raetz went on to make two slightly larger versions a few years later. It is characteristic of his appropriations of his own work that more than a decade elapsed between his abstract canvas reliefs and his reprise of their form—with a new thematic focus and in a different medium—as from 1977. In the mid-1960s, parallel to his canvas reliefs, Raetz had also executed a number of cut-out panels whose silhouettes are congruent with their graphically conceived motifs. For these colorfully painted sculptures cut out of wood panels, however, he chose other subjects.

17
Torso, 1978
(Fragment von / of *Zone blanche* / *White Zone*, 1965)
Acryl auf ungrundierter Leinwand / Acrylic on unprimed canvas, 124 x 52 cm
Nachlass / Estate of Markus Raetz, Bern

18
Torso, 1977
Kalkstein (?) / Limestone (?), 3,4 x 1,4 x 0,4 cm
Nachlass / Estate of Markus Raetz, Bern

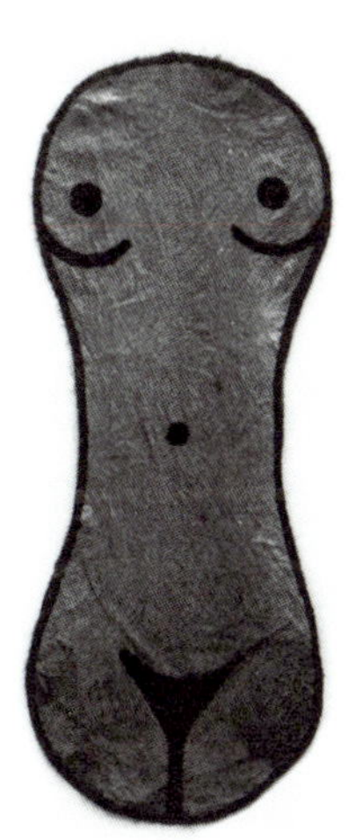

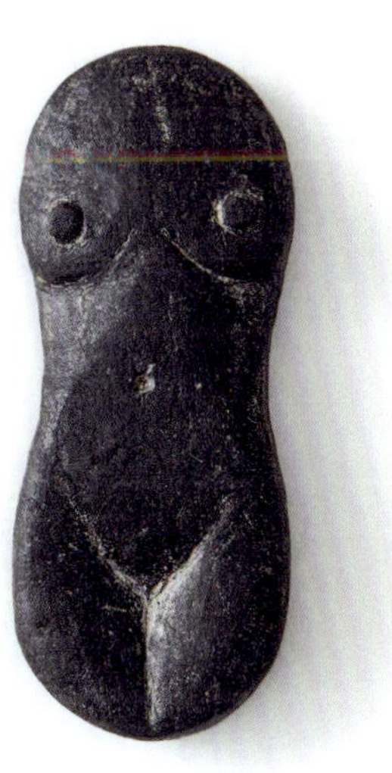

zität durch die Polsterung der Leinwand mit Schaumstoff zustande kommt. Gemeinsam ist den beiden Typen die hybride Medialität: Die Gesamtform und die Leinwand entsprechen dem traditionellen Gemälde, der Verzicht auf den Einsatz von Buntfarben und die hervortretenden Volumen gehören jedoch dem skulpturalen Bereich an. Die Position zwischen den Medien und das Changieren zwischen zwei- und dreidimensionaler Erscheinung sollten das gesamte Schaffen von Markus Raetz prägen und auch für *Zeemansblik* konstitutiv werden. Gleichzeitig entstandene gerahmte Reliefs aus Kautschuk-Noppenmatten mit zwei nebeneinanderliegenden kugeligen Ausstülpungen gehören ebenfalls in diesen Kontext (Abb. 15). Auf *Zeemansblik* weist neben ihrer formalen Struktur der industrielle Charakter der Kautschukmatten voraus, der sie mit dem üblicherweise im Bau eingesetzten und ebenso kunstfremden Titanzink verbindet.

In den erwähnten gepolsterten Leinwandreliefs erfuhr die Doppelkreisform schon eine erste Veränderung. Zum einen ist sie hier senkrecht ausgerichtet, zum anderen auch zur Drillingsfigur erweitert. Sie ist gelängt, weist mit den seitlichen Einbuchtungen eine harmonisch ondulierende Kontur auf und ähnelt nun einer Erdnuss[51] oder einem weiblichen Torso. Der Übergang zu einer figürlichen Bestimmung hatte die Freistellung der ungegenständlichen Form aus der bildhaften Fläche zur Folge. Beispielhaft zeigte sich der Prozess der skulpturalen Verselbstständigung einer ursprünglich grafischen Figur bei *Zone blanche* von 1965, der grössten Ausführung eines monochromen Polsterreliefs, dessen zentrales Feld Raetz herauslöste und mit wenigen aufgemalten Linien zum Torso eines weiblichen Akts umwidmete (Abb. 16, 17).[52] Er wies einer Form also einerseits verschiedene inhaltliche Aspekte zu, andererseits konnte eine als interessant erachtete Ikonografie in verschiedenen Materialien realisiert werden. In der Zeit, als er das grosse Leinwandfragment als Torso definierte, gestaltete er eine winzige Steinskulptur mit dem gleichen Motiv in identischer Form (Abb. 18). Sie weist jedoch, einer Rundplastik ähnlich, eine Rückseite auf, die ebenfalls bearbeitet ist. Zwei geringfügig grössere Fassungen entstanden wenige Jahre später. Es ist charakteristisch für Raetz' Appropriationen des eigenen Schaffens, dass die Reprise der Form, die mit einer neuen thematischen Ausrichtung einherging, und ihr medialer Wandel erst ab 1977 erfolgten, also mehr als ein Jahrzehnt nach der Entstehung der abstrakten Leinwandreliefs. Cut-out-Panels, deren Silhouetten mit ihren grafisch aufgefassten Motiven kongruent sind, hatte er Mitte der 1960er

Genesis of the Form: The Motif of the Binocular Field of View

In his monograph published in 1977, Jürgen Glaesemer emphasized the fundamental importance of drawing for Raetz. It was as natural to the artist as language, and synonymous with his thinking and actions; indeed, in the continuous flow of drawings he produced, it was part of life itself.[53] Raetz's drawing—in particular in the books he produced between 1972 and 1976—served as an artistic diary. The themes and motifs of his entire future œuvre are already contained in this almost overwhelmingly wide-ranging store of ideas. Drawing was the medium in which Raetz reflected on the representability of body and space: "Drawing is almost always the first step—including in the case of sculptures. What leads to them leads via drawing."[54] Here Raetz was, of course, alluding to the illusionistic representation of three-dimensional objects and space on a two-dimensional plane. Even more so, however, he was pointing to the fundamental motivation for his sculptural œuvre in general, namely the drive to lend concrete form, as sculpture, to drawing itself and to its basic elements of line and plane: "It was an old wish of mine to be able to draw in space. That was probably a motive for creating *Eva*: to set down a line in space."[55] Just as the 1970 elm-branch sculpture *Eva* (fig. 19) mentioned here by Raetz is without doubt the key work among his many linear sculptures, so *Zeemansblik* equally indisputably exemplifies the plane that has become sculpture. By extending lines and planes into space and lending them material substance, Raetz significantly expanded the scope of the concept of drawing. Its territory intersects with that of sculpture and to a great extent merges with it—or sculpture even claims it entirely for itself.

As with each of his sculptural works, Markus Raetz prepared the shape of *Zeemansblik* in countless drawings, showing all its preliminary stages, its actual and possible variations, and further developments. He sketched some of these ideas long before the work was executed as a relief (something not intended at the start). Other drawings were produced at or around the same time as the sculpture itself. Many can be linked only vaguely to a specific sculptural project, or not at all. The form of the overlapping circular discs, for example, appears in a 1975 book of drawings, on a sheet bearing the date May 10.[56] The intersection of the two circles here corresponds to a kayak, while the circles themselves represent the symmetrical ripples caused by the paddle. Six months

19
Eva, 1970/1980
3 Ulmenzweige, geschält, Plastilin /
3 elm branches, de-barked, modeling clay,
links / left: 38 cm, Mitte / middle: 22,5 cm,
rechts /right: 37 cm (Höhe / height),
Konsole: Ahornholz /
console: maple, 7,7 x 50 x 8 cm
Privatbesitz / Private collection

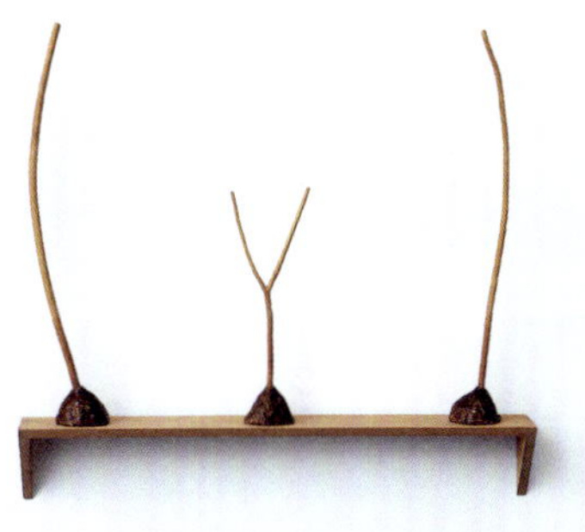

Jahre parallel zu den Leinwandreliefs auch schon ausgeführt, für die bunt gefassten hölzernen Scheibenplastiken wählte er jedoch andere Sujets.

Genese der Form: das Motiv des binokularen Blickfeldes

In seiner 1977 erschienenen Monografie wies Jürgen Glaesemer auf die grundlegende Bedeutung der Zeichnung für Raetz hin. Sie sei für ihn so selbstverständlich wie die Sprache und mit seinem Denken und Handeln, ja im kontinuierlichen Fluss der zeichnerischen Produktion seinem Leben gleichzusetzen.[53] Seine Zeichnung – nicht nur, aber in besonderem Mass in den von 1972 bis 1976 entstandenen Büchern – hatte die Funktion eines künstlerischen *journal intime*. In diesem geradezu überwältigend umfangreichen Fundus ist das thematische und motivische Repertoire seines gesamten zukünftigen Schaffens schon vorhanden. Dazu gehört auch, dass die Zeichnung das Medium war, in dem Raetz über die Darstellbarkeit von Körper und Raum reflektierte: «In jedem Fall ist Zeichnen fast immer der erste Schritt – auch bei den Skulpturen. Was zu ihnen führt, führt über die Zeichnung.»[54] Raetz sprach mit dieser Aussage natürlich die illusionistische Darstellung von dreidimensionalen Objekten und Raum auf der Fläche an. Weit mehr noch deutete er aber auf den essenziellen Antrieb für sein skulpturales Schaffen überhaupt hin, nämlich die Zeichnung selbst bzw. ihre Grundelemente Linie und Fläche als Skulptur zu konkretisieren. «Im Raum zeichnen zu können, war ein alter Wunsch von mir. Wahrscheinlich war das auch ein Motiv für die Entstehung von *Eva*: eine Linie in den Raum zu setzen.»[55] Wenn die hier von Raetz erwähnte Zweigplastik *Eva* von 1970 (Abb. 19) also ohne Zweifel das Schlüsselwerk seiner vielen linearen Skulpturen ist, so steht *Zeemansblik* ebenso unbestreitbar beispielhaft für die Skulptur gewordene Fläche. Mit der Verleihung von materieller Substanz und dem Ausgreifen von Linien und Flächen in den Raum erweiterte Raetz den Geltungsbereich des Zeichnungsbegriffs wesentlich. Er überschneidet sich mit demjenigen der Skulptur, verschmilzt weitgehend mit ihm, oder sie, die Skulptur, beansprucht ihn gar für sich.

Die Gestalt von *Zeemansblik* mit all ihren Vorstufen, ihren tatsächlichen und möglichen Variationen und Weiterentwicklungen bereitete Markus Raetz wie jedes skulpturale Werk in unzähligen Zeichnungen vor. Einige Ideen skizzierte er lange vor einer ursprünglich gar nicht intendierten skulpturalen Ausführung, andere entstanden in ihrer unmittelbaren zeitlichen Nachbarschaft.

20
Ohne Titel / Untitled, Detail einer Seite aus einem Zeichnungsbuch von 1975, Doppelseite datiert 18.11. / Detail of a page from a 1975 sketchbook, double page dated 18.11. Nachlass / Estate of Markus Raetz, Bern

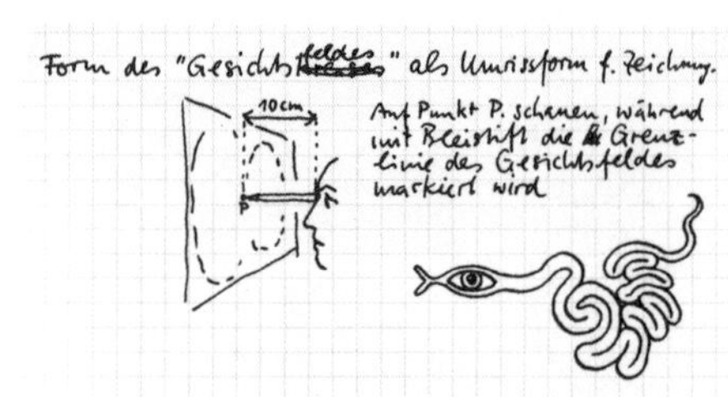

later, on November 18, 1975, Raetz assigned the double-circle figure possibly for the first time the significance of the binocular field of view so crucial with regard to *Zeemansblik*. The small sketch in question shows a pencil connecting the eye of a head with a pictorial plane represented in perspective, on which a double circle can be seen (fig. 20). The tip of the pencil is touching the "P" marking the center of the double circle. The accompanying shorthand note reads: "Form of the 'field of view' as outline form f[or] drawing. Look at point P while the boundary line of the field of view is marked with a pencil."[57] Raetz probably found inspiration for the motif in a well-known illustration in the book *Die Analyse der Empfindungen und das Verhältnis des Physischen zum Psychischen* by the physicist and philosopher Ernst Mach (1838–1916).[58] The illustration shows the view as seen through the author's left eye: in his field of view, bounded by his eyebrow, nose, and moustache, he can observe his drawing hand capturing his own torso and legs in foreshortening. Raetz had paraphrased almost the same view of his own body in a drawing of 1973, albeit without citing the characteristic form of the limited field of perception.[59] In his drypoint etching *Sehfeld* of 1986, the artist's hand holding the etching needle appears in a binocular pictorial field characteristic of *Zeemansblik*.[60] In 1992, Raetz made explicit reference to Mach's analyses of the physical senses in his work *Silhouetten (für Ernst Mach)*, the catoptric sculptural anamorphosis of a head.[61]

It seems to have been ten years before Raetz took up the motif of the binocular field of view in his drawings once more—in other words, at the exact same time as producing the first *Zeemansblik* versions. He thereby subjected the graphic element to a series of metamorphoses and opened it up to a broad spectrum of possible uses in terms of content. In the context of its aforementioned association with the female torso, he related the horizontally aligned form to the female bust. In a drawing of 1985, a male head gazes upon it.[62] Gilbert Lascault wrote of this sheet: "Here, everything is set in motion by approximative similarities between the observer and the observed. The eyes are shaped approximately like breasts; the nipple roughly corresponds to the pupil of an eye. To a certain extent, M. R. points to a kind of basic harmony between the person who desires and the focus of their desire."[63] Raetz's drawings —thus Lascault—express "a logic of analogy, not a logic of identity."[64] On another sheet, the binocular sea view and the torso are even directly related to each

21
Sammlung / Collection, 1985
Tinte auf Papier / Ink on paper,
21×30 cm
Nachlass / Estate of Markus Raetz, Bern

22
Ohne Titel / Untitled, 1985
Tinte auf Papier/ Ink on paper,
21×30 cm (?)
Nachlass / Estate of Markus Raetz, Bern

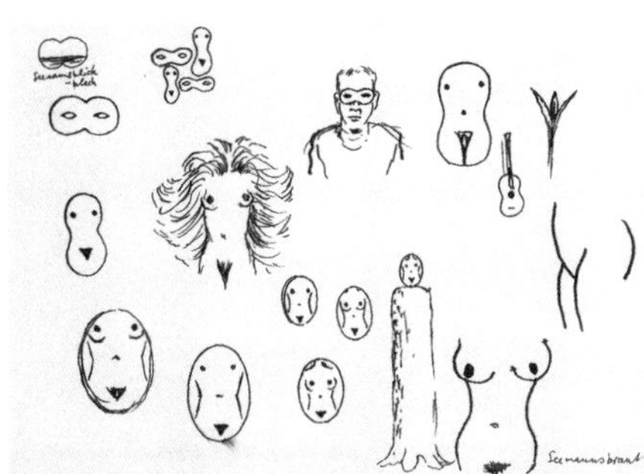

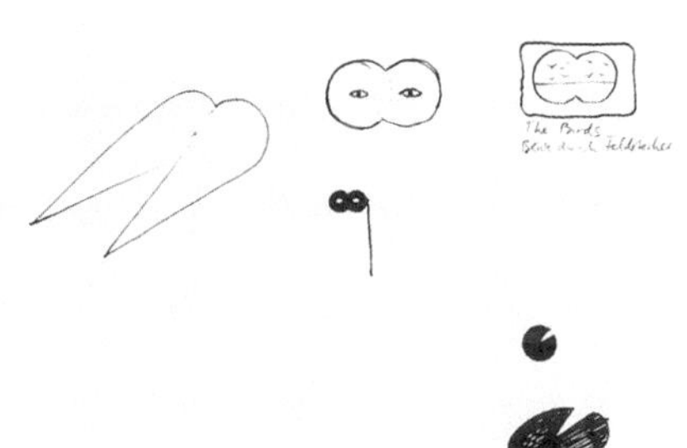

Sehr viele lassen sich nur vage oder gar nicht mit einem bestimmten skulpturalen Projekt in Verbindung bringen. So erscheint die Form der sich überschneidenden Kreisscheiben in einem Zeichnungsbuch von 1975 auf einem Blatt mit dem Datum 10. Mai.[56] Die Schnittfläche der beiden Kreise entspricht hier einem Kajak, die Kreise selbst stellen die vom Paddel verursachten symmetrischen Wellen dar. Ein halbes Jahr später, am 18. November 1975, wies Raetz der Doppelkreisfigur womöglich zum ersten Mal die im Hinblick auf *Zeemansblik* entscheidende Bedeutung des binokularen Gesichtsfeldes zu. Die kleine Skizze zeigt einen Stift, der das Auge eines Kopfes mit einer perspektivisch dargestellten Bildfläche verbindet, auf der ein Doppelkreis zu sehen ist (Abb. 20). Dessen mit «P» bezeichnetes Zentrum wird von der Spitze des Stifts berührt. Die dazugehörige Notiz lautet: «Form des ‹Gesichtsfeldes› als Umrissform f. Zeichnung. Auf Punkt P schauen, während mit Bleistift die Grenzlinie des Gesichtsfeldes markiert wird.»[57] Eine Anregung für das Motiv fand Raetz wohl in der berühmten Illustration im Buch *Die Analyse der Empfindungen und das Verhältnis des Physischen zum Psychischen* des Physikers und Philosophen Ernst Mach (1838–1916).[58] Sie zeigt das durch Braue, Nase und Schnurrbart begrenzte Gesichtsfeld des linken Auges, in dem die darin sichtbare zeichnende Hand des Schauenden seinen eigenen Torso und seine Beine in perspektivischer Verjüngung festhält. Raetz hatte den fast gleichen Blick auf seinen Körper in einer Zeichnung von 1973 paraphrasiert, allerdings ohne die charakteristische Form des begrenzten Wahrnehmungsbereichs zu zitieren.[59] In der Kaltnadelradierung *Sehfeld* von 1986 erscheint die Hand des Künstlers mit der Radiernadel schliesslich in einem binokularen Bildfeld, wie es für *Zeemansblik* charakteristisch ist.[60] 1992 wies Raetz explizit auf die sinnesphysiologischen Untersuchungen von Mach hin, als er ihm die katoptrische plastische Anamorphose eines Kopfes mit dem Werktitel *Silhouetten (für Ernst Mach)* widmete.[61]

Es scheint zehn Jahre gedauert zu haben, bis Raetz das Motiv des binokularen Gesichtsfeldes in seinen Zeichnungen wieder aufgriff, also genau zur Zeit der Entstehung der ersten *Zeemansblik*-Fassungen. Dabei unterzog er das grafische Element einer Reihe von Gestaltveränderungen und öffnete es für ein breites Spektrum der inhaltlichen Anwendungsmöglichkeiten. Im Kontext der schon erwähnten Assoziation mit dem weiblichen Torso bezog er die Form in horizontaler Ausrichtung auf die weibliche Büste. Auf einem Blatt von 1985 blickt ein männlicher Kopf darauf.[62] Gilbert Lascault schrieb dazu: «Hier wird alles durch appro-

other. The two motifs are corresponding labeled "Seemannsblick/-blech" ("Sailor's view / tin") and "Seemannsbraut" ("Sailor's bride") (fig. 21).[65] Raetz explored a further approximative similarity or analogy with the mask—a motif, in other words, that correlates with the field of view and effectively acts as its projection onto the face of the person looking out from behind it.[66] It lends the wearer anonymity: for the person exposed to their gaze, it thus makes them an invisible voyeur, so to speak, and the ultimate watcher. By partially concealing the face, the mask emphasizes the eyes and makes them appear isolated, like autonomous beings. In 1976, Raetz had already painted the black silhouette of an eye mask onto a mirror.[67] Whoever looks into it is viewed by their masked self. The subject of the eye mask may have been inspired by René Magritte, who represented the motif prominently in several of his paintings. It was the attribute of Fantômas, the main character in the popular French crime novel series of the same name, and a criminal as intelligent and cunning as he was ruthless. Magritte treated the fictional Fantômas in his art on a number of occasions. An egocentric creativity that played an important role in the Surrealists' universe of ideas expressed itself in Fantômas' asocial behavior and almost exquisite evil, and made him a dazzling figure of identification for avant-garde artists in the interwar period.[68] The eye mask was part of his appearance as an outlaw with the attitude of a dandy, not only on book covers but also in movie series made at an early date. The Bern-born Art Brut artist Adolf Wölfli (1864–1930) was a real-life social outsider of great creativity. The face costumed with an eye mask appears in many variations in his repertoire of motifs, probably in the sense of self-portrayals. Raetz included it in his short compendium of Wölfli's formal vocabulary, compiled in 1996.[69]

In one of his drawings of July 1985 with mask variations, Raetz finally identified the motif of the binocular field of view as a view through field glasses of the sea-level horizon.[70] The small, vignette-like sketch in the top right-hand corner of the sheet shows the double-circle figure in outline within a rectangle, as if this were the representation of a picture-within-a picture (fig. 22). The field of view is lent structure by a continuous horizontal line and a number of small curved segments above it, which in the context of the outlined shape we recognize as a horizon line and birds in flight. Beneath the drawing, Raetz wrote: "The Birds / Blick durch Feldstecher" ("The Birds / View through field glasses").

ximative Ähnlichkeiten zwischen dem Betrachter und dem Betrachteten in Gang gebracht. Die Augen haben ungefähr die Form von Brüsten, der Warze entspricht in etwa [der] Augapfel. M. R. weist gewissermassen auf eine Art Grundharmonie zwischen dem Begehrenden und dem Begehrten hin.»[63] In seinen Zeichnungen äussere sich «eine Logik der Analogie und nicht eine der Identität».[64] Auf einem anderen Blatt sind der binokulare Meerblick und der Torso sogar unmittelbar aufeinander bezogen. Die entsprechenden Motive sind bezeichnet mit «Seemannsblick/-blech» und «Seemannsbraut» (Abb. 21).[65] Eine weitere approximative Ähnlichkeit oder Analogie zeigte Raetz mit der Maske auf, einem Motiv also, das mit dem Gesichtsfeld korreliert und wie seine Projektion auf das Gesicht des Blickenden wirkt.[66] Sie verleiht ihm Anonymität und macht ihn für das Gegenüber, das seinem Blick ausgesetzt ist, gleichsam zum unsichtbaren Voyeur, dem Schauenden schlechthin. Die das Gesicht partiell kaschierende Rahmung betont die Augen und lässt sie isoliert wie autonome Wesen erscheinen. Raetz hatte die schwarze Silhouette einer Augenmaske schon 1976 auf einen Spiegel gemalt.[67] Wer in ihn blickt, wird von seinem maskierten Ich betrachtet. Für das Sujet der Augenmaske könnte René Magritte Pate gestanden haben, der sie in mehreren Bildern prominent in Szene gesetzt hat. Sie war das Attribut der ihn wiederholt beschäftigenden Titelfigur der populären französischen Kriminalromanserie *Fantômas*, eines so intelligenten und raffinierten wie skrupellosen Verbrechers. Im asozialen Handeln und in der geradezu exquisiten Bösartigkeit von Fantômas äussert sich eine egozentrische Kreativität, die eine wichtige Rolle in der Gedankenwelt der Surrealisten spielte und ihn zu einer schillernden Identifikationsfigur von Avantgardekünstlern in der Zwischenkriegszeit machte.[68] Zu seiner nicht nur auf den Buchumschlägen, sondern auch schon früh in Filmserien geprägten Erscheinung des Outlaws mit der Attitüde eines Dandys gehörte die Augenmaske. Ein realer gesellschaftlicher Aussenseiter von grosser Kreativität war der Berner Art-Brut-Künstler Adolf Wölfli (1864–1930). In seinem motivischen Repertoire taucht das mit einer Augenmaske kostümierte Gesicht wohl im Sinn von Selbstdarstellungen in vielen Varianten auf. Raetz nahm sie in sein kleines Kompendium von Wölflis Formenvokabular auf, das er 1996 anlegte.[69]

Auf einer der Zeichnungen vom Juli 1985 mit den Maskenvariationen präzisierte Raetz das Motiv des binokularen Gesichtsfeldes schliesslich als Blick durch ein Fernglas auf den Meereshorizont.[70] Die vignettenhaft kleine Skizze in

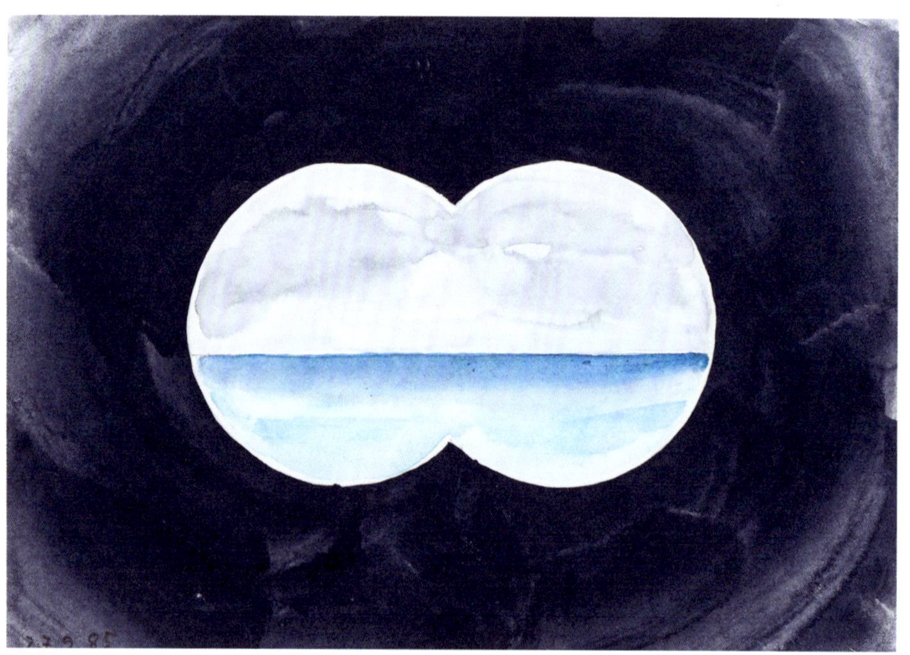

It is therefore clear that the series of *Zeemansblik* reliefs on which he embarked in this period represent not simply the vista opening up before the eyes of a person looking across the surface of the water, but the narrowed view seen through field glasses. Raetz's caption furthermore hints at the spectrum of iconographic sources for this familiar and in itself unassuming motif: *The Birds* is the title of a classic 1963 movie by Alfred Hitchcock. A still from *The Birds*, showing the field of view framed in black with a scene from the movie, is reproduced in the catalog of Raetz's 1988 exhibition in Venice. In the history of cinema and in comics, this type of image has become a commonplace means of representing an observer whom we do not see but whose view we share, thus translating us into the role of observer ourselves. The formal forerunners of the binocular field of view in Raetz's œuvre, namely his purist abstract reliefs of the 1960s, were rooted in the conceptual and aesthetic tradition of Constructivism and Minimalism. With his assignment of specific content-related functions to the double-circle figure,

23
Ohne Titel / Untitled, 1985
Aquarell auf Papier / Watercolor on paper,
10,5 × 14,7 cm
Nachlass / Estate of Markus Raetz, Bern

der rechten oberen Ecke des Blatts zeigt die Doppelkreiskontur innerhalb eines Rechtecks, als würde hier ein Bild im Bild wiedergegeben (Abb. 22). Strukturiert ist das Blickfeld durch eine durchlaufende waagrechte Linie und eine Anzahl kleiner Bogensegmente darüber, die wir im Zusammenhang mit dem Umriss als Horizontlinie und Vögel im Flug erkennen. Unter die Zeichnung notierte Raetz: «The Birds / Blick durch Feldstecher». Damit steht fest, dass die gleichzeitig einsetzende Reihe der *Zeemansblik*-Reliefs nicht einfach darstellt, was sich den Augen eines über die Wasserfläche schauenden Menschen eröffnet, sondern den eingeengten Blick durch ein Fernglas. Die Unterschrift deutet darüber hinaus das Spektrum der ikonografischen Anregungen für das vertraute und an sich anspruchslose Motiv an: *The Birds* war der Titel eines Filmklassikers von Alfred Hitchcock aus dem Jahr 1963. Ein Still daraus, der das schwarz eingefasste Blickfeld mit einer Szene des Films zeigt, ist im Katalog von Raetz' Ausstellung in Venedig 1988 abgebildet. Dieser Bildtyp hat sich in der Filmgeschichte und im Comic zu einem Gemeinplatz entwickelt für die Darstellung eines Beobachters, den wir nicht sehen, an dessen Beobachtung wir aber teilhaben und dadurch selbst in die Rolle der Beobachtenden versetzt werden. Die formalen Ahnen des Fernglasblickfelds im Werk von Raetz, die erwähnten puristisch abstrakten Reliefs der 1960er Jahre, standen in der konzeptuellen und ästhetischen Tradition der konstruktiven Kunst und der Minimal Art. Mit der Zuweisung spezifischer inhaltlicher Funktionen an die Doppelkreisfigur fand eine Öffnung des Referenzfeldes zur figurativen Pop-Art und schliesslich in den Bereich der Alltags- und Populärkultur statt. Unabhängig vom Medium – Comicstrip, Film, Foto, Gebrauchsgrafik – bot sich dort ein breites Angebot an unmittelbar einleuchtenden formalen Lösungen für die Vermittlung von Inhalten. «Mir gefällt an den Cartoons vor allem die Reduktion aufs Wesentliche, die Tatsache, dass man mit wenigen Strichen etwas erzählen kann», fasste Raetz seine Wertschätzung für diese Bereiche der visuellen Gestaltung zusammen.[71]

Die zwei Jahrzehnte dauernde, medienübergreifende Evolution der Doppelkreiskontur zur signetartigen Silhouette des Fernglasblickfelds weist sie als eines der zentralen Elemente in Raetz' Motivspektrum aus. Dass die fast beliebige Austauschbarkeit von Objektbezügen einer Form und folglich die «Konstituierung eines objektbezogenen Vokabulars» grundlegend für Raetz' Kunst sei, stellte Jean-Christophe Ammann schon Ende der 1960er Jahre fest.[72]

24
Escalet II, 1985
Öl auf Sperrholz / Oil on plywood,
18,8 × 90,6 × 0,7 cm
Nachlass / Estate of Markus Raetz, Bern

his field of reference now opened up to figurative Pop Art and ultimately to the realm of everyday and popular culture. Here lay a broad range of formal solutions that enabled content to be communicated in an instantly illuminating way, whatever the medium—whether comic strip, film, photography, or commercial art. "What I like about cartoons first and foremost is their reduction to the essentials, the fact that you can tell a story with just a few strokes," said Raetz, summing up his appreciation of these areas of visual design.[71]

The evolution—over two decades and in multiple media—of the double-circle figure in outline into the signet-like silhouette of the binocular field of view proclaims it as one of the central elements in Raetz's spectrum of motifs. The almost arbitrary interchangeability of the objects to which a form could make reference, and consequently the "constitution of an object-related vocabulary," was identified by Jean-Christophe Ammann as early as 1968 as being fundamental to Raetz's art.[72] In Ammann's view, this included cylinders, tubes, faces in profile, waves, grid structures, clouds, and hilly horizons, which take shape first as drawings before being deployed in sculpture. Looking back over Raetz's œuvre as a whole, we may also add the perspective representation of cuboids. As argument that this was a "real vocabulary," Ammann cited "the ability of the objects to be used and their ability to change in different contexts."[73] In order for the field-of-vision form to be usable as a *Zeemansblik*, it needed the context of the seascape.

Genesis of the Motif: The Horizon Line and the Non-Painted Seascape

Writing about landscape in Raetz's work, Stephan Kunz noted that landscape and nature represent two of the artist's most important points of orientation when developing his visual concepts.[74] In the early 1970s, Raetz's interest was

25
Escalet VI, 1985/1989
Öl auf Buchenholz / Oil on beech,
19,2×92×1,1 cm
Nachlass / Estate of Markus Raetz, Bern

Dazu zählten in seiner Sicht Kugelzylinder, Schläuche, Gesichtsprofile, Wellen, Gitterstrukturen, Wolken und Hügelhorizonte, die zuerst als Zeichnungen Gestalt annehmen, bevor sie skulptural eingesetzt werden. Im Rückblick auf sein gesamtes Schaffen muss man auch die perspektivische Darstellung von Quadern hinzufügen. Als Argumente dafür, dass es sich dabei um ein «wirkliches Vokabular» handelt, nannte Ammann «die Verwendbarkeit der Objekte, ihre Veränderungsfähigkeit in verschiedenen Zusammenhängen».[73] Für die Verwendbarkeit der Blickfeldform als *Zeemansblik* war der Kontext der Meerlandschaft notwendig.

Genese des Motivs: die Linie des Horizonts und die nicht gemalte Meerlandschaft

Die Landschaft und die Natur gehören «zu den wichtigsten Orientierungspunkten bei der Entwicklung seines bildkünstlerischen Konzepts», stellte Stephan Kunz in einem Aufsatz über die Landschaft im Werk von Raetz fest.[74] In den frühen 1970er Jahren waren es vor allem die Phänomene des Wassers und der Wüste, die ihn interessierten. Naturalistische Veduten von Küstenlandschaften und wiederum Darstellungen von Wasser und Wolken in Bleistift und Aquarell gestaltete Raetz vor allem ab Mitte der 1970er Jahre und wieder Mitte der 1980er Jahre, als die *Zeemansblik*-Reihe entstand. Auch das Fernglasblickfeld mit dem Motiv des Meereshorizontes malte er zu dieser Zeit in Aquarell (Abb. 23). Gleichzeitig verknappte er das marine Sujet in Malereien auf kleinen, oblongen Holztafeln zu einem Diagramm aus seitlich ins Bildfeld ragenden Dreiecken, die eine besonnte und eine beschattete Klippe repräsentieren, und auf eine horizontale Teilung in Meer und Himmel. Bei einigen Tafeln ist die Herkunft von der abbildenden Vedute noch ersichtlich in der Andeutung der stofflichen Eigenschaften von Fels, Wasser und Luft. Andere präsentieren sich ohne Kenntnis ihrer Genese als

directed above all at the phenomena of water and the desert. He produced naturalistic *vedute* of coastal landscapes and representations of water and clouds in pencil and watercolor, most notably from the mid-1970s and again in the mid-1980s, when the *Zeemansblik* series took shape. The binocular field of view with the motif of the horizon of the sea also appears in a watercolor from the mid-1980s (fig. 23). During this same period, in paintings executed on small, oblong wooden panels, he reduced the marine subject to a diagram consisting of triangles projecting into the pictorial field from the right- and left-hand side and representing one sunlit cliff and one in the shade, and to a horizontal division into sea and sky. In some of these panels, their roots in representational *vedute* are still evident in the suggestion of the material properties of rock, water, and air. Without knowing their genesis, however, others present themselves as abstract, Constructivist compositions that simulate a geometric body rather than the depth of space (figs. 24, 25). The purist form of the constructed landscape motif, and the object-like character of these paintings, place them in direct relation to the *Zeemansblik* reliefs. Five of the six versions were created in January 1985, parallel to the reliefs made of folded paper mentioned earlier. The small series is named after L'Escalet, a section of the French Mediterranean coast with rocky coves and a small harbor. It belongs to the municipality of Ramatuelle,[75] which Raetz and his wife first visited in 1967 and where for many years, from 1977 onwards, they spent several weeks a year. While the Dutch title of the sheet-metal reliefs forges a link with the North Sea, the L'Escalet motif refers to the Mediterranean and thus to another important location in Raetz's biography.

Landscape, perhaps more than any other of the traditional genres of visual art, relies on drawing or painting as a medium. As early as the mid-1960s, however, Raetz created reliefs out of wood comprising landscape elements in radically simplified form. They represent the fleeting phenomena of waves and clouds that fundamentally refuse to be fixed in sculpture, and which would later determine *Zeemansblik*. In this latter, however, the silhouette of the relief is no longer identical with these landscape elements of variable form, and the landscape appears upon it merely as an immaterial image. It requires the sculptural means of the horizontal fold to conjure this image onto the blank sheet metal at all. The fold is the only element structuring the surface, and marks the horizon line. Raetz did not place this "magical section through all dimensions, on which

ungegenständliche, konstruktivistische Kompositionen, die weniger die Tiefe des Raums vortäuschen als einen geometrischen Körper (Abb. 24, 25). Die puristische Form des konstruierten Landschaftsmotivs und der objekthafte Charakter stellen diese Malereien in den unmittelbaren Zusammenhang mit den *Zeemansblik*-Reliefs. Fünf der sechs Fassungen entstanden im Januar 1985, parallel zu den erwähnten Reliefs aus gefalzten Papieren. Die kleine Serie ist nach L'Escalet benannt, einem Abschnitt an der französischen Mittelmeerküste mit felsigen Buchten und einem kleinen Bootshafen. Er gehört zur Gemeinde Ramatuelle,[75] wo Raetz und seine Frau erstmals 1967 und ab 1977 für längere Zeit jährlich mehrere Wochen verbrachten. Während der niederländische Titel der Blechreliefs einen Bezug zur Nordsee herstellt, verweist die Herkunft des darauf sichtbaren Motivs also auf das Mittelmeer und damit auf eine weitere wichtige biografische Station von Raetz.

Die Landschaft ist wie wohl keine andere der traditionellen bildkünstlerischen Gattungen auf das Medium der Zeichnung und Malerei angewiesen. Aber schon Mitte der 1960er Jahre hatte Raetz Reliefs aus Holz mit stark abstrahierten landschaftlichen Versatzstücken gestaltet. Es handelt sich ausgerechnet um die flüchtigen, sich einer skulpturalen Fixierung prinzipiell verweigernden Phänomene von Wellen und Wolken, die auch wieder für *Zeemansblik* bestimmend werden sollten. Hier ist die Silhouette des Reliefs aber nicht mehr identisch mit diesen formvariablen Elementen der Landschaft, die lediglich als immaterielles Bild darauf erscheinen. Um es auf dem blanken Blech überhaupt hervorzubringen, brauchte es das skulpturale Mittel des waagrechten Falzes. Er ist das einzige Element, das die Fläche strukturiert, und markiert die Horizontlinie. Dass Raetz diesen «magischen Schnitt durch alle Dimensionen, an dem sich die Reflexionen als Phänomene des Lichtes wie des Geistes brechen»,[76] trotz der suggestiven Symmetrie der Silhouette nicht auf die waagrechte Mittelachse setzte, sondern die Fläche im Goldenen Schnitt in Meer und Himmel unterteilte, verstärkt die bildhafte Wirkung zusätzlich. Die Situierung des Horizonts auf der natürlicher wirkenden, unteren Goldenen Linie assoziiert die Reliefs mit der langen Tradition der Landschafts- und Marinemalerei. Auch das Verhältnis von der Höhe zur Breite des Reliefs entspricht dem Goldenen Schnitt. Es ist nicht auszuschliessen, dass es sich hier um eine mehr intuitiv gewählte als mathematisch konstruierte Komposition handelt. Wenige Monate nach der Entstehung des

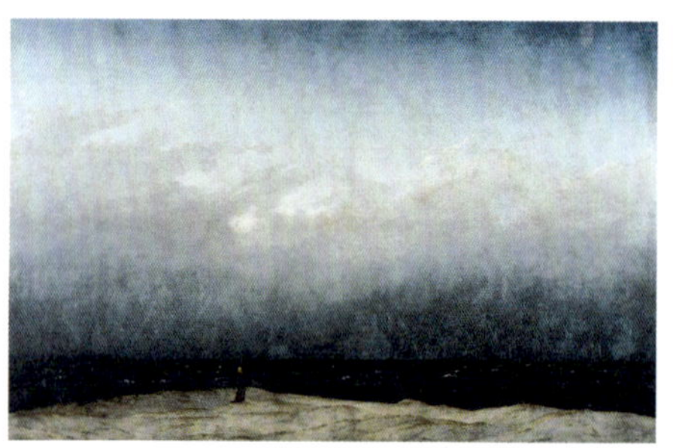

26
Caspar David Friedrich
Der Mönch am Meer / The Monk by the Sea, 1808–1810
Öl auf Leinwand / Oil on canvas, 110 × 171 cm
Alte Nationalgalerie, Berlin

the reflections refract as phenomena of light and intellect,"[76] on the horizontal center line, despite the suggestive symmetry of the silhouette. Instead, he divided the surface into sea and sky in the golden ratio, further enhancing the impression that we are looking at a picture. The siting of the horizon on the lower, more natural-looking golden-ratio dividing line associates the reliefs with the long tradition of landscape and marine painting. The ratio of the height to the width of the relief likewise corresponds to the golden ratio. The possibility that this composition was intuitively chosen rather than mathematically calculated cannot be ruled out. A few months after creating the Aarau *Zeemansblik*, however, Raetz employed this traditional formula in a conscious and consistent manner. In his *Nächtliches Seebild*, a work with an identical motif and whose pictorial effect is generated by the minimal relief of the surface of unpainted buckskin, the dimensions of height and width and the position of the horizon follow the Fibonacci numbers.[77] The proportions thus correspond approximately to the golden ratio. Raetz adopted this compositional principle in the later versions of *Zeemansblik*, too.

The horizon line represents the minimum necessary to allow the image of a landscape to appear on a blank surface. In *Zeemansblik*, the restriction of the iconography to this single element, which itself has neither extension nor volume and which separates the infinite surface of the sea from the infinite space of the sky, fosters the impression of sublimity. In this context, it is tempting to think of Heinrich von Kleist (1777–1811) and his oft-cited description of the painting *The Monk by the Sea* (1808–1810) by Caspar David Friedrich (1774–1840) (fig. 26). Lending expression to the viewer's horror before the emptiness of the almost unstructured seascape, in 1810 Kleist wrote: "And since [this painting], in its monotony and boundlessness, has nothing but its frame as foreground, it is, when you look at it, as if your eyelids had been cut away."[78] Even if, in *Zeemansblik*, Raetz made explicit reference neither to Friedrich's painting nor to its literary reception by Kleist, the landscape painting of Romanticism played a role for him. He was particularly interested in British artists, especially John Constable (1776–1837), who is known for his naturalistic studies of skies and clouds. In Raetz's opinion, the subject of clouds is of comparable importance in the history of painting as the representation of drapery, since both motifs afforded "scope for invention."[79] In his drawings of the first half of the 1970s,

Aarauer *Zeemansblik* wandte Raetz dieses traditionelle Schema jedoch bewusst und konsequent an. Beim motivisch identischen *Nächtlichen Seebild*, bei dem die Bildwirkung durch das minimale Relief der Oberfläche von unbemaltem Wildleder zustande kommt, folgen die Masse von Höhe und Breite und die Lage des Horizonts den Fibonacci-Zahlen.[77] Die Proportionen entsprechen damit annähernd dem Teilungsverhältnis des Goldenen Schnitts. Auch bei den späteren Fassungen von *Zeemansblik* entschied sich Raetz für dieses Kompositionsprinzip.

Die waagrechte Horizontlinie repräsentiert das notwendige Minimum, um auf einer leeren Fläche das Bild einer Landschaft erscheinen zu lassen. Die Beschränkung des ikonografischen Angebots auf dieses einzige Element, das selbst keine Ausdehnung besitzt und die unendliche Fläche des Meeres vom unendlichen Raum des Himmels trennt, fördert bei *Zeemansblik* den Eindruck von Erhabenheit. Es ist in diesem Zusammenhang verführerisch, Heinrich von Kleists (1777–1811) oft zitierte Beschreibung von Caspar David Friedrichs (1774–1840) Gemälde *Der Mönch am Meer* (1808–1810) heranzuziehen (Abb. 26). Darin verlieh Kleist dem Erschrecken des Betrachters vor der Leere der fast unstrukturierten Meerlandschaft Ausdruck: «[...] und da es [das Bild], in seiner Einförmigkeit und Uferlosigkeit, nichts, als den Rahm, zum Vordergrund hat, so ist es, wenn man es betrachtet, als ob einem die Augenlider weggeschnitten wären.»[78] Auch wenn Raetz sich bei *Zeemansblik* weder explizit auf Friedrichs Gemälde noch auf dessen literarische Rezeption durch Kleist bezog, spielte die Landschaftsmalerei der Romantik für ihn eine Rolle. Sein Interesse galt dabei vor allem den englischen Künstlern, insbesondere John Constable (1776–1837), der für seine naturalistischen Himmel- und Wolkenstudien bekannt ist. Raetz' Meinung nach ist das Sujet der Wolke in der Geschichte der Malerei von vergleichbarer Bedeutung wie die Darstellung von Faltenwürfen, da beide Motive «Spielraum zum Erfinden» gewährten.[79] So entwickelte er in der ersten Hälfte der 1970er Jahre aus parallelen, sich ondulierend entfaltenden Linien fantastische Landschaftsszenerien in seinen Zeichnungen. Für die Genese von *Zeemansblik* spielte das Blotting-Verfahren des englischen Landschaftsmalers Alexander Cozens (1717–1786) eine wichtige Rolle.[80] In seiner Abhandlung *A New Method of Assisting the Invention in Drawing Original Compositions of Landscape* von 1785/86, die Raetz kannte, beschrieb er die Methode, von Flecken (englisch: *blots*) auf dem Papier und Knitterfalten ausgehend Fantasielandschaften zu konstruieren: «[...] es ist ein Verfah-

he thus developed fantastical landscape scenes out of parallel, undulating lines. The method of blotting used by the British landscape painter Alexander Cozens (1717–1786) played an important role for the genesis of *Zeemansblik*.[80] In his 1785/86 treatise *A New Method of Assisting the Invention in Drawing Original Compositions of Landscape*, with which Raetz was acquainted, Cozens wrote of his method of constructing fantasy landscapes from blots of ink and creases on the paper: "Composing landscapes by invention is not the art of imitating individual nature; it is more; it is forming artificial representations of landscape on the general principles of nature, founded in unity of character, which is true simplicity."[81] Cozens saw an advantage of his method in the fact that blots could suggest different ideas to different viewers. His theory, he wrote, was "the art of seeing properly."[82]

Raetz distanced himself, however, from the Romantic leaning towards the emotional state of the sublime. In *Zeemansblik*, he ironized the pathos formula of the unbounded seascape with his use of mundane sheet metal and the pop-cultural subject of the binocular field of view, which thwarts the impression that the limits of perception have been entirely removed. While the silhouette and the horizon line of *Zeemansblik* have a static, geometric character, its surface reveals new impressionistic painterly effects at every moment, in keeping with the transitory nature of the motif. Without the slightest use of paint, these are generated simply by the changing incidence of light on the matte reflective surface of the sheet metal.[83] Jean-Luc Monterosso called the relief "a seascape without painting."[84] Marcia Tucker drew attention to the contradictory and complex nature of *Zeemansblik*'s medium when she wrote that "perhaps the most pervasive series of 'landscape' paintings in [Raetz's] œuvre are neither landscapes nor paintings, but pieces of cut and bent tin."[85] In 2014, Raetz explained his reluctance to use color in his sculptures on the grounds that he had dedicated himself from an early date primarily to form, and ultimately had "an insufficiently intimate relationship to color" to be able to call himself a painter.[86] This in no way meant renouncing pictures, however. He simply delegated painting in this case to the sculptural form, the material, and the light—and to our *musée imaginaire* of seascapes.

Also belonging to the canon of marine imagery are the Seascape photo paintings by Gerhard Richter (b. 1932), which were produced from the

27
Gerhard Richter
Seestück (bewölkt) / Seascape (Cloudy), 1969
Öl auf Leinwand / Oil on canvas, 200 x 200 cm
Neues Museum – Staatliches Museum für Kunst und Design in Nürnberg, Leihgabe der Sammlung / on loan from Collection Böckmann, Berlin

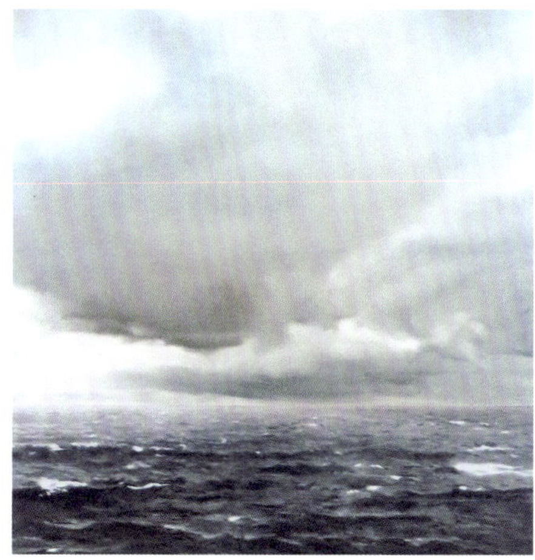

ren, künstliche Darstellungen von Landschaft aus den generellen Prinzipien der Natur zu formen, gegründet in der Einheit des Charakters, der in wahrer Einfachheit besteht [...].»[81] Einen Vorteil seiner Methode sah Cozens darin, dass die *blots* bei den Betrachtenden unterschiedliche Vorstellungen hervorrufen können. Seine Theorie sei «die Kunst, genau zu sehen».[82]

Dem Hang der Romantiker zur Gefühlslage der Erhabenheit stand Raetz aber distanziert gegenüber. Er ironisierte die Pathosformel der unbegrenzten Meerlandschaft bei *Zeemansblik* mit der Verwendung von profanem Blech und dem populärkulturellen Sujet des Fernglasblickfeldes, das den Eindruck der völligen Entgrenzung der Wahrnehmung konterkariert. Während der Umriss von *Zeemansblik* und die Linie des Horizonts einen statischen, geometrisch-grafischen Charakter besitzen, offenbaren sich auf seiner Oberfläche in jedem Moment neue impressionistisch-malerische Effekte, die dem transitorischen Wesen des Motivs gerecht werden. Hervorgerufen werden sie ohne den geringsten Einsatz von Malfarbe allein durch den wechselnden Lichteinfall auf der matt spiegelnden Oberfläche des Blechs.[83] «Ein Marinebild ohne Malerei» nannte Jean-Luc Monterosso das Relief.[84] Und Marcia Tucker machte auf die mediale Widersprüchlichkeit und Komplexität von *Zeemansblik* aufmerksam, wenn sie schrieb, dass es sich bei den Landschaftsgemälden mit der grössten Resonanz in Raetz' Werk weder um Landschaften noch um Gemälde handle.[85] Er habe sich schon früh in erster Linie der Form verschrieben und habe letztlich «ein zu wenig intimes Verhältnis zur Farbe», als dass er sich als Maler bezeichnen könne, begründete Raetz 2014 seine Zurückhaltung in der Verwendung von Farben bei seinen Skulpturen.[86] Das bedeutete aber keineswegs den Verzicht auf Bilder. Er delegierte in diesem Fall das Malen lediglich an die plastische Form, das Material und das Licht – und an unser Musée imaginaire der gemalten Seestücke.

Zum kanonischen Bestand der marinen Bilder gehören auch die *Seestücke* von Gerhard Richter (*1932), die ab Ende der 1960er und Mitte der 1970er Jahre entstanden und *Zeemansblik* zeitlich wesentlich näherstehen als die Bilder der Romantiker (Abb. 27). Wie Caspar David Friedrich griff Richter dabei unverhohlen das auf die niederländische Malerei des 17. Jahrhunderts zurückgehende Schema der seitlich offenen, panoramatisch weiten Landschaft mit tief liegendem Horizont und leerem Vordergrund auf und verzichtete auf eine abwechslungsreiche, harmonisch ausgewogene Komposition.[87] Denn dieser traditionsreiche

late 1960s and mid-1970s, and are consequently much closer to *Zeemansblik* in time than the works of the Romantics (fig. 27). Like Caspar David Friedrich, Richter openly took up the formula—dating back to seventeenth-century Dutch painting—of the panoramic landscape unbounded at the sides, with a low horizon and empty foreground, and dispensed with a varied, harmoniously balanced composition.[87] This traditional formula namely provided the elements crucial for the modernization of landscape painting in the post-war period. The reduction to two parts with one above the other, which the motif of the sea-level horizon demands, lends a picture a very high degree of abstraction—something to which the all-over structure of the sea's surface also contributes. In order to emphasize the self-referential character of his painting, and to further minimize the representational quality of the motif, which latter is reproduced distinctly out of focus, Richter based the zones of sea and sky on photographs that in most cases did not belong together. Through this subtle manipulation, any stirring of the emotions at the sight of the paintings loses all meaning. Richter's analytical approach to the medium was his reaction to the postulate that contemporary conceptual art spelled the end of painting. Raetz had himself pursued conceptual approaches at the end of the 1960s and in 1969 participated in Harald Szeemann's now legendary show *Live in Your Head: When Attitudes Become Form* at the Kunsthalle Bern—a formative moment for conceptual art. With *Zeemansblik*, he accomplished the feat of responding to the demands of conceptual art and at the same time paying his respects to the great but scorned tradition of painting. Without having to pick up a brush, Raetz, like Richter, celebrated painterly refinement and at that same time complied with the latter's call for a subject-less painting. The fact that the painterly landscape leading away into the infinite depths before our eyes in *Zeemansblik* is only the reflection of the floor and ceiling is part of his ironically subversive play with art-historical references, ideological demands on a medium, and our expectations. The physical boundaries of the exhibition space allow us to see on the relief the blue distance, as beautiful as if it were painted.[88]

Typus bot die entscheidenden Elemente für die Aktualisierung der Landschaftsmalerei in der Nachkriegszeit. Die Reduktion auf zwei übereinanderliegende Teile, welche das Motiv des Meereshorizonts fordert, verleiht einem Bild einen sehr hohen Grad der Abstraktion, zu dem auch die All-over-Struktur der Meeresoberfläche beiträgt. Um den selbstreferenziellen Charakter seiner Malerei zu betonen und die Abbildhaftigkeit des extrem unscharf wiedergegebenen Motivs noch weiter zu minimieren, verwendete Richter für die Himmelszone und das Meer meistens nicht zusammengehörende fotografische Vorlagen und liess durch diese subtile Verfremdung jede sentimentale Regung bei der Betrachtung der Gemälde ins Leere laufen. Der analytische Umgang mit dem Medium war Richters Reaktion auf das vor dem Hintergrund der zeitgenössischen Konzeptkunst postulierte Ende der Malerei. Raetz hatte Ende der 1960er Jahre selbst konzeptuelle Ansätze verfolgt und 1969 an Harald Szeemanns legendär gewordener Ausstellung *Live in Your Head: When Attitudes Become Form* in der Berner Kunsthalle – einem Schlüsselereignis der Konzeptkunst – teilgenommen. Mit *Zeemansblik* brachte er das Kunststück zustande, den Anliegen der Konzeptkunst zu entsprechen und sich zugleich vor der grossen, aber verpönten Tradition der Malerei zu verneigen. Ohne zum Pinsel greifen zu müssen, zelebrierte er wie Richter malerisches Raffinement und kam dabei dessen Forderung einer «subjektlosen Malerei» nach. Zu seinem ironisch subversiven Spiel mit kunstgeschichtlichen Referenzen, ideologischen Ansprüchen an ein Medium und unseren Erwartungen gehört auch, dass der malerische Landschaftsraum, der sich auf *Zeemansblik* vor unseren Augen unendlich weit in die Tiefe öffnet, nur der Widerschein von Boden und Decke ist. Die physischen Begrenzungen des architektonischen Raums lassen uns auf dem Relief die blaue Ferne sehen, schön wie gemalt.[88]

Seh-Räume: die Ikonografie der visuellen Wahrnehmung und das Motiv der Landschaft

«On peut regarder [voir] voir; on ne peut pas entendre entendre.» Diesen Satz notierte Marcel Duchamp 1914 auf einen Zettel. Ob Markus Raetz ihn kannte, ist ungewiss, aber gut möglich. Zusammen mit 15 weiteren handschriftlichen Notizen und einer Zeichnung veröffentlichte ihn Duchamp 1914 als fotografisches Faksimile.[89] Spätestens seit der von Harald Szeemann kuratierten Ausstellung *Junggesellenmaschinen* von 1975, in der Duchamps sogenanntes *Grosses*

28
Ohne Titel / Untitled, 1985
Ölkreide auf Papier / Oil pastel on paper, 20,9×29,9 cm
Nachlass / Estate of Markus Raetz, Bern

29
Ohne Titel / Untitled, 1985
Chinesische Füllfeder und Tinte auf Papier / Chinese fountain pen and ink on paper, 20,9×29,9 cm
Nachlass / Estate of Markus Raetz, Bern

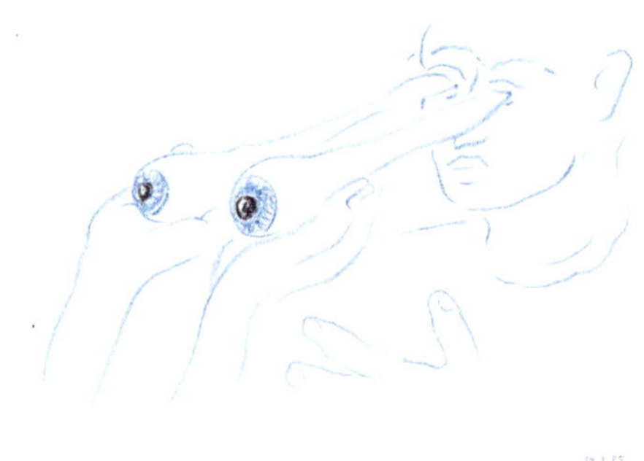

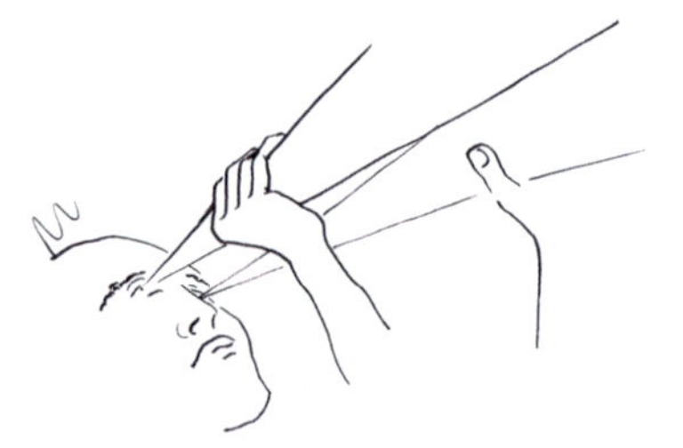

"Seeing-Spaces": The Iconography of Visual Perception and the Landscape Motif

"On peut regarder [voir] voir; on ne peut pas entendre entendre" ("One can look at seeing but one can't hear hearing"). Marcel Duchamp jotted down this sentence on a piece of paper in 1914. Whether Markus Raetz was familiar with it is uncertain, but quite possible. Duchamp published the handwritten note, along with fifteen others and a drawing, as photographic facsimiles that same year.[89] At the latest from the 1975 exhibition *Junggesellenmaschinen* curated by Harald Szeemann,[90] in which Duchamp's so-called *Large Glass* took center stage and in which Raetz also participated with drawings, Raetz knew Duchamp's work and repeatedly paid homage to it. In addition to his creative appropriation, discussed earlier, of the work title *Why not Sneeze, Rose Sélavy?*, Raetz chose a motif cited by Duchamp from a painting by Paul Delvaux (1897–1994) as the subject for an entire sculptural work group,[91] and as late as 2011 paraphrased a Duchamp *Self-Portrait in Profile* collage in a wire sculpture.[92] His interest in hanging sculptures and kinetics may also have been inspired by Duchamp. The motif of looking through the openings of caves and portholes, which Duchamp used repeatedly and which also appears in many variations in Raetz's work, is particularly significant in our context. It served both artists as a visual metaphor for the process of seeing. The visibility of seeing asserted by Duchamp in his note is the prerequisite for its representability. Raetz shifted the focus from neutral seeing to mindful looking and summed up his visualized thought processes about visual perception in the phrase "das Beobachten des Beobachtens"—"the observation of observation."[93]

Representations of the sense organs as embodiments of the senses are found in Raetz's drawings from an early date, with the sense of sight thereby assuming greatest importance. The binocular field of view made up of two overlapping circles is part of a wide-ranging iconography of visual perception that plays a fundamental role in Raetz's work. This iconography includes the eye and the gazing head and is usually represented in combination with the eyebeam and the pyramid or cone of vision. This latter is the cone around the eyebeam, with the pupil as its apex. Projected onto a two-dimensional plane, this cone of vision has the shape of an isosceles triangle. The pyramid or cone of vision is an auxiliary geometric construct for simulating three-dimensionality on

30
Kluge Kugel III / Intelligent Ball III, 1985–1986
Aquatinta (Zuckertusche-Absprengverfahren) / Sugar-lift aquatint, 21 x 26 cm
Nachlass / Estate of Markus Raetz, Bern

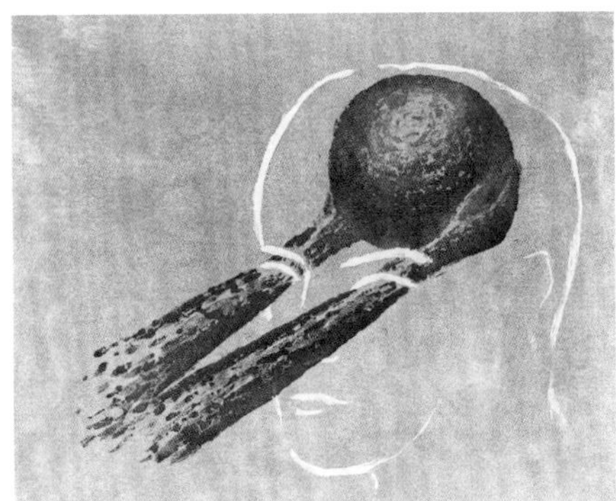

Glas im Zentrum stand und an der Raetz mit Zeichnungen teilnahm,[90] war Raetz mit Duchamps Werk vertraut und erwies ihm wiederholt die Reverenz. Neben der schon erwähnten kreativen Aneignung des Werktitels *Why not Sneeze, Rose Sélavy?* wählte er ein Motivzitat Duchamps nach einem Detail aus einem Gemälde von Paul Delvaux (1897–1994) als Sujet für einen ganzen skulpturalen Werkkomplex[91] und paraphrasierte noch 2011 eine Selbstbildnis-Collage Duchamps in einer Drahtplastik.[92] Sein Interesse für Hängeplastiken und die Kinetik mag ebenfalls durch Duchamp angeregt worden sein. In unserem Zusammenhang ist besonders das Motiv des Durchblicks durch Öffnungen von Höhlen und Bullaugen bedeutsam, das Duchamp wiederholt verarbeitete und das auch bei Raetz in vielen Variationen vorkommt. Es diente beiden als bildliche Metapher für den Vorgang des Sehens. Die in Duchamps eingangs zitiertem Satz behauptete Sichtbarkeit des Sehens ist die Voraussetzung für dessen Darstellbarkeit. Raetz verschob den Fokus vom neutralen Sehen zum reflektierten Betrachten und fand für seine visualisierten Denkprozesse über die visuelle Wahrnehmung die Formel «das Beobachten des Beobachtens».[93]

In seinen Zeichnungen finden sich schon früh Darstellungen der Sinnesorgane als Verkörperungen der Sinne. Die grösste Bedeutung kommt dabei dem Sehsinn zu. Das binokulare Blickfeld aus zwei verschränkten Sehkreisen ist Teil einer breitgefächerten Ikonografie der visuellen Wahrnehmung, die in seinem Werk eine fundamentale Rolle spielt. Dazu gehören das Auge und der blickende Kopf. Meist stellte Raetz sie in Kombination mit dem Sehstrahl und der Sehpyramide bzw. dem Sehkegel dar. Der Sehkegel ist der Konus um den Sehstrahl, dessen Spitze den Augpunkt markiert. Auf die Fläche projiziert hat er die Form eines gleichschenkligen Dreiecks. Die Sehpyramide bzw. der Sehkegel ist eine geometrische Hilfskonstruktion zur Simulation von Dreidimensionalität auf einer Fläche, das heisst zum perspektivisch korrekten Bild eines Körpers und des Raums. Raetz entliess ihn aus der Unsichtbarkeit seiner dienenden Aufgabe und adelte ihn zum eigenständigen Sujet mit dem Status eines Leitmotivs, das für den Prozess des Sehens schlechthin steht. In seinen Zeichnungen wies er dem auf diese Weise Bild gewordenen Sehvorgang den gleichen Stellenwert zu wie den blickenden Köpfen und den Motiven, die sie ins Auge fassen. Er unterzog den Sehkegel nicht nur wie die Blickfeld-Silhouette vielfältigsten Gestaltveränderungen, sondern verlieh ihm die physische Präsenz eines Körpers oder sogar eines

31
Doppelkonus / Double Cone, 1986/2005
Buchenholz, schwarz gebeizt und gewachst, 2-teilig / Beech, stained black and waxed, 2-part, 17 x 24 x 59 cm
Nachlass / Estate of Markus Raetz, Bern

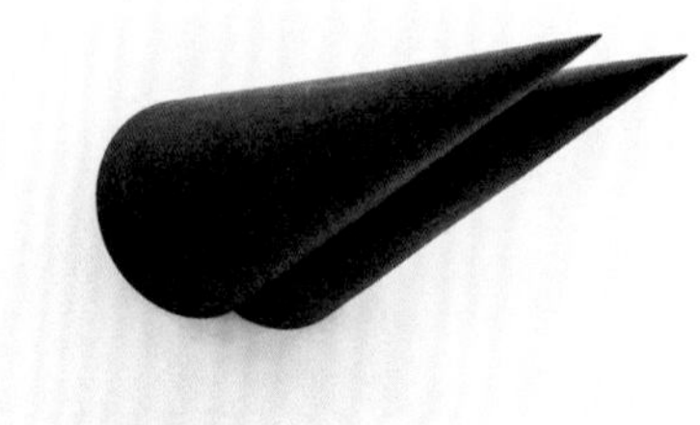

a plane, i.e., for creating a correct perspective image of a body and space. Raetz released it from the invisibility of its serving role and elevated it to an independent subject, granting it the status of a leitmotif that stands for the process of seeing per se. In his drawings, he attached the same importance to the process of seeing visually represented in this way as to the gazing heads and the motifs at which they are looking. Raetz not only rendered the cone of vision, like the silhouette of the field of view, in a wide variety of forms, but even lent it the physical presence of a body or a living thing. It thus appears as a grotesque, mobile protrusion of the eyeball (fig. 28), as something branching like a tree out of the eye sockets, as a long, pointed needle, as a cloud of smoke, and as the cone of light from a spotlight. The most common variants are those in which the gazing person holds the cones of vision in their hands, as if they were a pair of field glasses (fig. 29).[94] Raetz represented seeing as a distinctly sensual, physical, and consequently synesthetic experience, in which it is not always clear whether the experience emanates from the person or comes to meet them, as in the sheets titled with the German anagram *Kluge Kugel* (*Intelligent Ball*). Here, hands reach from the outside through the eye sockets into the skull and clasp the brain (fig. 30).[95] Exploiting the possibilities reserved for the medium of drawing, and with a lack of concern for realism adopted from the comic strip, Raetz furnished the opposing historical concepts of extramission and intromission with the same visual evidence. These two theories of vision, which were developed in ancient Greece and remained influential right up to the Middle Ages, were based on two contrary premises. According to the first, the eye emits a beam—of whatever substance—in order to perceive the environment (extramission), while according to the second, objects emit images of themselves that penetrate our eyes in materialized form (intromission).[96] Seeing is thereby awarded a tactile property, literally in the sense of grasping what is visually perceived or of being grasped by what is seen.

It seems logical that Raetz should not only help his leitmotif of the binocular cone of vision achieve visibility in his drawings, but also lend it material form in his wood sculpture *Doppelkonus* of 1986 (fig. 31).[97] Three decades later, he returned to the cone motif in free-hanging sculptural objects made of sheet aluminum.[98] The side view of an installation floating in space like a cloud, made up of numerous wire sculptures individually set in motion by drafts of air,

32
Ohne Titel (Wolke) / Untitled (Cloud), 2020
Skizze für eine Installation aus hängenden Drahtplastiken mit Segeln aus Aluminiumblech, Bleistift auf Papier / Sketch for an installation of suspended wire sculptures with sails of sheet aluminum, pencil on paper
20,9 × 29,9 cm
Nachlass / Estate of Markus Raetz, Bern

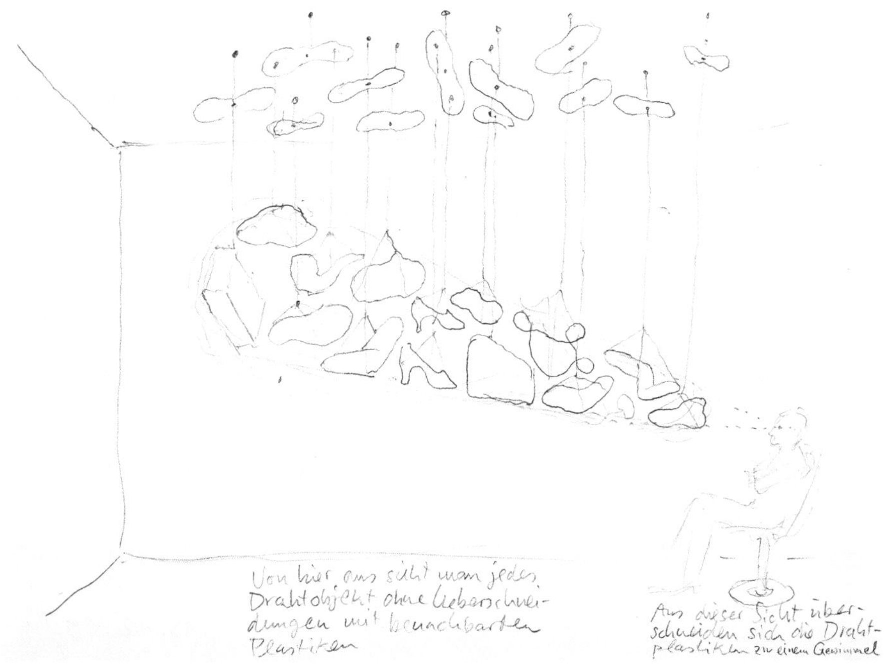

lebendigen Wesens. Er erscheint als groteske, bewegliche Ausstülpung des Augapfels (Abb. 28), als von den Augenhöhlen ausgehende baumartige Verzweigung, als lange, spitze Nadel, als Rauchwolke und als Lichtkegel eines Scheinwerfers. Am häufigsten sind die Varianten, bei denen der blickende Mensch die Sehkegel in den Händen hält, als wären sie ein Fernglas (Abb. 29).[94] Raetz stellte das Schauen als eine ausgesprochen sinnliche und körperliche, mithin als eine synästhetische Erfahrung dar, bei der nicht immer klar wird, ob sie von den Menschen ausgeht oder ihnen eher zustösst wie bei den mit dem Anagramm *Kluge Kugel* betitelten Blättern. Darauf greifen Hände von aussen durch die Augenhöhlen in den Schädel und umfassen das Gehirn (Abb. 30).[95] Mit den Möglichkeiten, die dem Medium der Zeichnung vorbehalten sind, und der vom Comic übernommenen Unbekümmertheit in Bezug auf den Realitätsgrad der Darstellung verlieh Raetz den gegensätzlichen historischen Wahrnehmungskonzepten der Extromission und der Intromission die gleiche bildliche Evidenz. Die Sehtheorien, die in der griechischen Antike entwickelt wurden und bis ins Mittelalter wirksam waren, beruhten auf zwei gegensätzlichen Prämissen. Der einen zufolge sendet das Auge einen – aus welcher Substanz auch immer bestehenden – Sehstrahl aus, um die Umwelt wahrzunehmen (Extromission), nach der anderen strahlen die Objekte Bilder von sich selbst aus, die in materialisierter Form in unsere Augen eindringen (Intromission).[96] Dem Sehen wird dabei eine taktile Eigenschaft zuge-

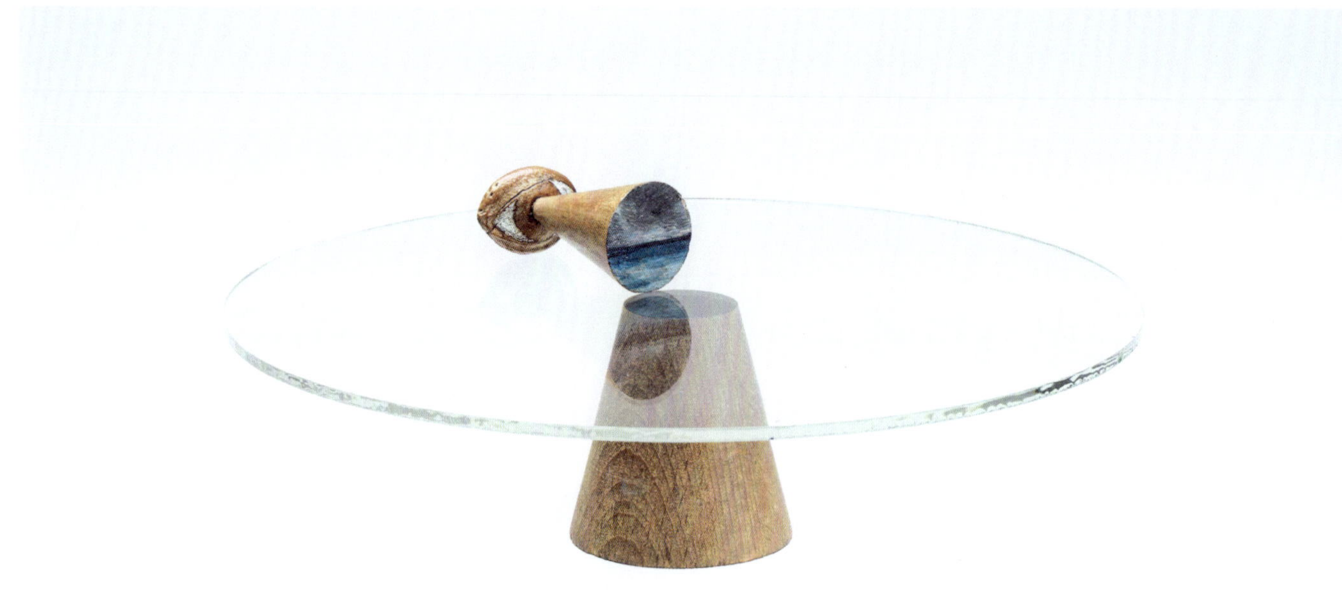

also corresponds to a cone, whose apex points at the eye of a person looking at it. The fact that Raetz conceived this installation in a number of drawings shortly before his death in April 2020, but did not live to see its execution, lends it the special status of his final work and thus the character of an artistic testament (fig. 32).[99]

The circle of vision is where the cone of vision intersects the pictorial plane. *Zeemansblik* represents the binocular view's two overlapping circles of vision isolated from the pictorial plane, and corresponds to the cross section of two cones of vision. The relief thus constitutes the complementary counterpart to *Doppelkonus*. A small multipart sculpture, likewise produced in 1986, brings together the separate elements of the cone and circle of vision and combines them with the gazing eye (fig. 33).[100] The seascape perceived by the eye is painted on the cross section of the wooden cone. The work's title, *Eye-cone*, is as ambiguous as the word *Zeemansblik*. As a compound, it names the two components of the work, i.e., the eye and the cone, and through its sound introduces the likewise English word "icon" into the mix. *Eye-cone* thus refers to the image perceived and moreover to the process of seeing discussed here, which it embodies—to pursue this idea a step further—in almost iconic fashion.

33
Eye-cone, 1986/1989
Aprikosenkern, bemalt, Ölfarbe auf Holz / Apricot kernel, painted, oil on wood, 2,4 × 2,7 × 5,1 cm, Holz / wood, 5 cm (Höhe / height), max. 5 cm (Ø), Glasscheibe / glass pane, 20 cm (Ø)
Nachlass / Estate of Markus Raetz, Bern

sprochen, und zwar buchstäblich, im Sinn des Begreifens des visuell Wahrgenommenen bzw. des vom Gesehenen Ergriffenseins.

Es erscheint konsequent, dass Raetz sein Leitmotiv des binokularen Sehkegels nicht nur in seinen Zeichnungen zur Sichtbarkeit verhalf, sondern mit dem *Doppelkonus* aus Holz von 1986 auch skulptural materialisierte (Abb. 31).[97] Drei Jahrzehnte später griff er das Motiv des Konus in mobilen Hängeplastiken aus Aluminiumblech wieder auf.[98] Auch die seitliche Ansicht einer wie eine Wolke im Raum schwebenden Installation aus zahlreichen Drahtplastiken, die sich einzeln im Luftzug bewegen, entspricht einem Konus, dessen Spitze auf das Auge einer betrachtenden Person zielt. Der Umstand, dass er diese Installation selbst zwar nicht mehr ausführen konnte, sie aber auf einigen Zeichnungen kurz vor seinem Tod im April 2020 noch konzipierte, verleiht ihr den besonderen Status des letzten Werks und damit den Charakter eines künstlerischen Testaments (Abb. 32).[99]

Der Sehkreis ist die Schnittfläche des Sehkegels auf der Bildebene. *Zeemansblik* repräsentiert die zwei aus der Bildebene isolierten, verschränkten Sehkreise des binokularen Blicks und entspricht der Schnittfläche von zwei Sehkegeln. Das Relief stellt somit das komplementäre Gegenstück zum *Doppelkonus* dar. Eine kleine mehrteilige Skulptur, die ebenfalls 1986 entstand, führt die separaten Elemente des Sehkegels und des Sehkreises zusammen und kombiniert sie mit dem blickenden Auge (Abb. 33).[100] Auf die Schnittfläche des hölzernen Konus ist das vom Auge wahrgenommene Marinebild gemalt. Der englische Titel *Eye-cone* ist von vergleichbarer Mehrdeutigkeit wie das Wort *Zeemansblik*. Die Fügung benennt die Werkbestandteile des Auges und des Sehkegels und verweist, das ebenfalls englische Wort *icon* über seinen Klang ins Spiel bringend, auf das wahrgenommene Bild und darüber hinaus auf den hier thematisierten Sehvorgang, der – so darf man den Gedanken weiterführen – auf geradezu ikonische Weise verkörpert ist.

Das miniaturhafte Marinebild ist in unserem Zusammenhang aufschlussreich, weil es zusammenfällt mit den ikonografischen Elementen, die für die visuelle Wahrnehmung stehen. Dies verbindet *Eye-cone* mit *Zeemansblik*. Markus Raetz kombinierte Darstellungen des Sehens oft mit der Landschaft. Meist handelt es sich um kleinformatige Malereien von Landschaftsausschnitten, seltener von Bergszenerien und mehrheitlich von Küsten- und Meermotiven.

34
Seeblick II / Sea View II, 1981/1985
6 Bruyèrezweige, 14 Holzstücke (Schwemmholz), bemalt (die meisten Ölfarbe) / 6 heather branches, 14 pieces of wood (driftwood), painted (the majority in oil)
55 × 222 cm
Privatbesitz / Private collection

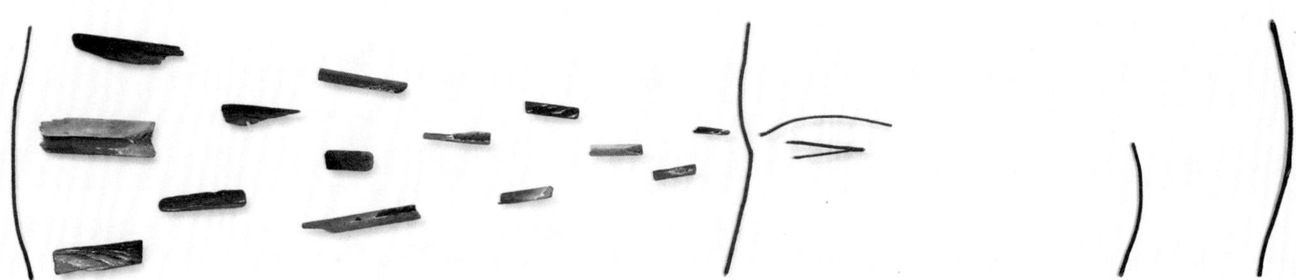

The miniature-like marine painting is revealing in our context because it is congruent with the iconographic elements that stand for visual perception. This links *Eye-cone* with *Zeemansblik*. Markus Raetz often combined representations of seeing with landscapes. These usually take the form of small-format paintings of landscape views, for the most part showing coastal and sea motifs and only infrequently mountain scenery. These fragments of *vedute* suggest rather than show, and so spark our imagination. In the versions of *Seeblick*, they represent the eye-beam or the triangular field of view and are combined with gazing heads— schematically indicated with twigs—into wall-mounted installations (fig. 34).[101] In a number of paintings on panels, the view of the sea through two cave mouths suggests the binocular view from inside the head, and not only amalgamates the theme of looking with the genre of landscape, but also marries the image of the interior chamber with the notion of the human skull and brain (fig. 35). The 1985 pictorial object *Die Galerie am Meer* transforms the motif of the anthropomorphic landscape into an enigmatic anthropomorphic architecture, in which a human eye looks out at us from a dark gallery.[102]

The works exploring these themes were created in the first half of the 1980s and hence are the forerunners of *Zeemansblik*. In 1983, Raetz for the first time devoted an entire exhibition gallery to this complex of motifs of seeing and landscape elements. In one of the rooms at the Kunstmuseum Bern, he combined small paintings, sculptures, and reliefs made of twigs into a

35
See-Stück / Sea Piece, 1983
Ölfarbe auf Sperrholz / Oil on plywood,
39 x 25,5 cm
Teil einer grossen Rauminstallation im /
part of a whole-room installation
at the Kunstmuseum Bern
Kunstmuseum Bern, Bern

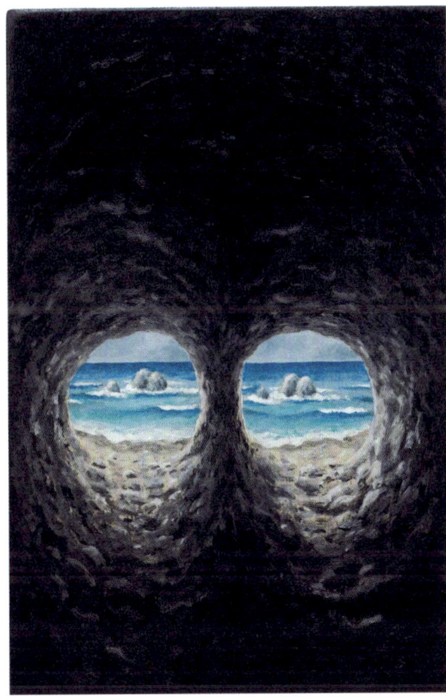

Die Fragmente von Veduten deuten mehr an als sie zeigen und fordern unsere Imagination heraus. Bei den Fassungen von *Seeblick* bilden sie den Sehstrahl oder das Dreieck des Blickfelds und fügen sich zusammen mit blickenden Köpfen aus Zweigen zu Wandinstallationen (Abb. 34).[101] Auf einigen Bildtafeln suggeriert der Ausblick aus zwei Höhlen auf das Meer den binokularen Blick aus dem Innern des Kopfes und führt nicht nur das Thema des Schauens mit dem Genre der Landschaft zusammen, sondern überblendet das Bild des Höhlenraums mit der Vorstellung des menschlichen Schädels und Gehirns (Abb. 35). Das Bildobjekt *Die Galerie am Meer* von 1985 transformiert das Motiv der anthropomorphen Landschaft in eine rätselhafte anthropomorphe Architektur, auf der uns ein menschliches Auge aus einem dunklen Korridor entgegenblickt.[102]

Die Werke mit dieser Thematik entstanden in der ersten Hälfte der 1980er Jahre und sind somit die Vorläufer von *Zeemansblik*. 1983 widmete Raetz erstmals einen ganzen Raum diesem Komplex aus Motiven des Sehens und der landschaftlichen Versatzstücke. Er fügte für einen Saal im Kunstmuseum Bern kleine Malereien, Skulpturen und Reliefs aus Zweigen zu einer suggestiven, offenen Bilderzählung, die vom Blick in die Weite der Landschaft zu introspektiven dunklen Visionen führt.[103] Das narrative Prinzip dieser Anordnung diente ihm in der Folge als Matrix für seine Werkpräsentationen, vor allem aber übernahm er für seine wichtigsten Ausstellungen bis Ende der 1980er Jahre ihr «alles andere als abstraktes Thema: Sehen».[104] In seine teils umfassenden Einzelausstellungen 1986 im Kunsthaus Zürich, in Köln und Stockholm, 1988 in New York und an der Biennale in Venedig und schliesslich 1989 in Basel integrierte er ein oder mehrere Exemplare von *Zeemansblik* in solche Arrangements. Dieter Koepplin bezeichnete sie als «Seh-Räume» und präzisierte, es seien «Wege des Sehens [...] in Räumen, die zugleich innen und aussen waren, zugleich Höhlen und weiteste Horizonte gaben».[105] Unter dem Begriff Horizont stellen wir uns, in seinen Worten, «am liebsten jenen schlichten, beruhigenden oder auch immer wieder aufwühlenden, dramatischen Meereshorizont vor, der die meditativen Romantiker ebenso in Bann zog wie die tatkräftigen Abenteurer».[106] Koepplins Fokus auf das Motiv des Meereshorizonts war gewiss *Zeemansblik* zu verdanken, von dem mehrere Fassungen in der Ausstellung gezeigt wurden und der dem ganzen Basler «Seh-Raum» den Titel gab. Angesichts von Raetz' Hang zur nicht nur formalen und ikonografischen Mehrdeutigkeit, sondern vor allem zur sprachlichen

36
Ensemble mit *Feldstechermann*-Exemplaren / Ensemble with examples of *Binocular Man*, 1987–1994, Atelier Markus Raetz, Bern, 2018

suggestive, open visual narrative that led from the view into the vast expanse of the landscape to introspective dark visions.[103] The narrative principle of this exhibit served Raetz as a matrix for his subsequent work presentations, and he adopted its "anything but abstract theme: seeing" for his most important exhibitions right up to the end of the 1980s.[104] He thus integrated one or more versions of *Zeemansblik* within such arrangements in his solo shows in 1986 at the Kunsthaus Zürich, Cologne, and Stockholm, in 1988 in New York and at the Venice Biennale, and lastly in 1989 in Basel. Dieter Koepplin described these self-contained rooms as "Sehräume" ("seeing rooms" or "rooms of vision"), and more specifically as "ways of seeing [...] in spaces that were simultaneously inside and outside, that simultaneously offered caves and farthest horizons."[105] According to Koepplin, what we picture under the term "horizon" is "most of all the flat and soothing, at other times roiling and dramatic sea-level horizon that cast its spell over meditative Romanticists and bold adventurers alike."[106] Koepplin's focus on the motif of the sea-level horizon was undoubtedly influenced by *Zeemansblik*, several versions of which were on show at the 1989 Basel exhibition. The show also featured two whole-room installations likewise titled *Zeemansblik*. In view of Raetz's penchant not only for formal and iconographic ambiguity, but above all for linguistic double meanings, it seems reasonable to imagine these "seeing rooms" as "sea rooms," too. The *Zeemansblik* reliefs as literal embodiments of the view of the sea-level horizon are the quintessence of the multi-part "seeing rooms" with their marine connotations.

***Zeemansblik* and *Feldstechermann*: The Visualization of the Perception of Landscape**

The *Zeemansblik* work group, as the synthesis of a major theme explored by Raetz in a wide range of motifs, marked the end of a development. But it was simultaneously the basis for new constellations of works. In 1987 and 1988, the years during which he executed the majority of the *Zeemansblik* versions, Raetz also produced an extensive group of small and very small *Feldstechermann* (*Binocular Man*) sculptures: variously made of wood, stone, and cast iron, brass and steel, they show a man looking through field glasses (fig. 36).[107] Within Raetz's central theme of the representability of visual perception, these "binocular men" embody the aspect of active observation. They are placed on tall,

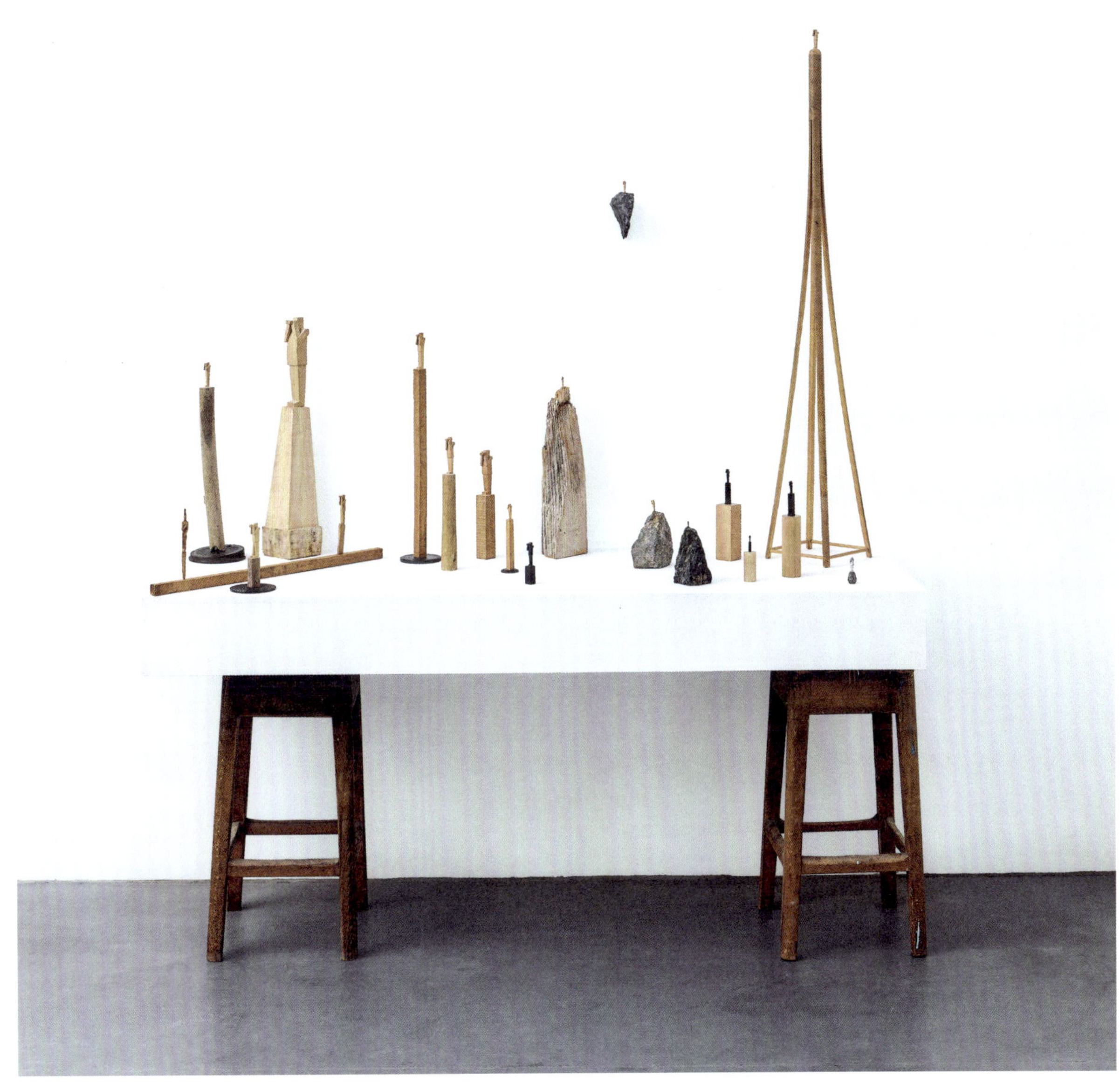

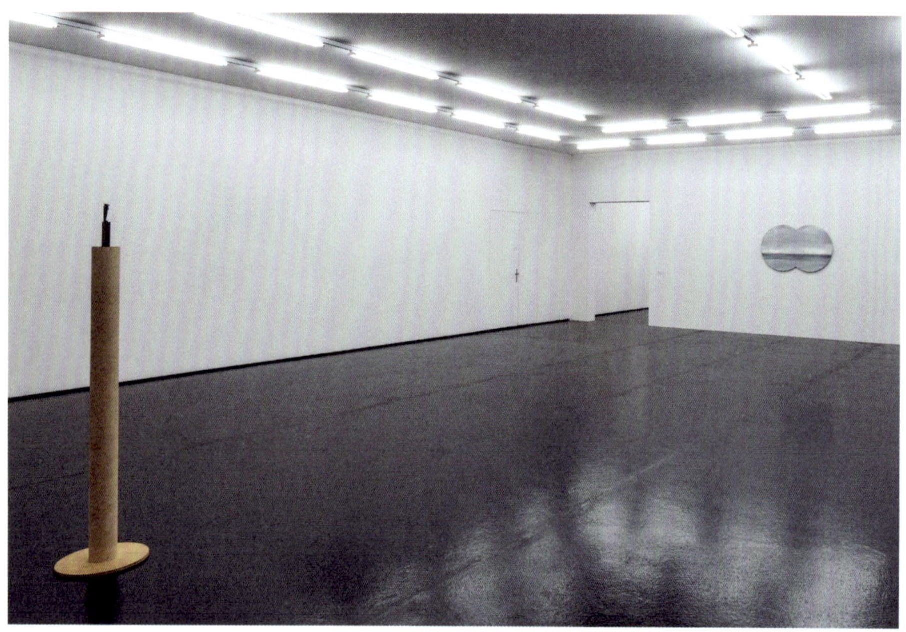

tower-like pedestals or stand on pieces of rock as if on a cliff or mountain top. The impression of breadth and distance inherent in the motif of the man looking through field glasses is heightened by this remote, isolated position on a high vantage point. Despite the figure's diminutive size, its hieratic verticality lends it a commanding presence, as also characteristic of the miniaturized sculptures by Alberto Giacometti (1901–1966), for example.

Since 1988, the *Feldstechermann* sculptures—often in small groups—have formed an inherent part of Raetz's whole-room installations. The sculptures usually appear as the pendant to a *Zeemansblik* relief and complement the latter's landscape representation to create an archetypal visualization of the perception of landscape. It is difficult not to think once again of Caspar David Friedrich's *Monk by the Sea*, his *Wanderer above the Sea of Fog* (1818), and other of his paintings in which a figure seen from behind in the foreground, representing ourselves as viewers, looks out into the vast landscape. But as Kleist sorrowfully confessed in his article of 1810, despite this offer of a figure

37
Installationsansicht mit *Fernsicht* / Installation view with *Distant View*, 1987/1994, Eisenguss / cast iron, 21,1×2,7×2,7 cm
Sockel: Kartonrohr / pedestal: cardboard tube, ca. 155 cm (Höhe / height), 18 cm (Ø), Ex. / no. 3/6, und / and *Zeemansblik*, 1987, Zinkblech, gefalzt / zinc sheet, folded, 83×134×4,4 cm, 0,1 cm (Stärke Blech / sheet thickness), im / at the Aargauer Kunsthaus, Aarau, 2021

Ambivalenz, liegt es nahe, sich diese «Seh-Räume» auch als «See-Räume» vorzustellen. Die *Zeemansblik*-Reliefs als buchstäbliche Verkörperungen des Blicks auf den Meereshorizont sind die Quintessenz der vielteiligen, marin konnotierten «Seh-Räume».

Zeemansblik und *Feldstechermann*: die Visualisierung der Landschaftsbetrachtung

Die Werkreihe von *Zeemansblik* bildete als Synthese eines motivisch weitverzweigten thematischen Schwerpunkts den Abschluss einer Entwicklung. Sie war aber zugleich die Grundlage neuer Werkkonstellationen. In den Jahren 1987 und 1988, parallel zur Mehrzahl der *Zeemansblik*-Fassungen, entstand eine umfangreiche Gruppe kleiner und kleinster Skulpturen aus Holz, Stein sowie Eisen-, Messing- und Stahlguss, die einen durch ein Fernglas schauenden Mann darstellen (Abb. 36).[107] Innerhalb von Raetz' Leitthema der Darstellbarkeit visueller Wahrnehmung verkörpern die *Feldstechermänner* den Aspekt des aktiven Beobachtens. Die Figuren sind auf hohen, turmartigen Sockeln platziert oder stehen auf Bruchsteinen wie auf einer Bergkuppe oder Klippe. Der entrückte Standort auf hoher Warte steigert den Eindruck von Weite, der im Motiv des Feldstechermanns angelegt ist, und seine hieratische Vertikale verleiht ihm trotz seiner geringen Dimension eine raumfordernde Präsenz, wie sie beispielsweise auch Alberto Giacomettis (1901–1966) fast volumenlosen Kleinplastiken eigen ist.

Seit 1988 gehören die *Feldstechermänner* – oft in kleinen Gruppen – zum selbstverständlichen Bestand der von Raetz eingerichteten «Seh-Räume». Meist treten die Skulpturen als das Gegenüber eines *Zeemansblik*-Reliefs auf und vervollständigen die Landschaftsdarstellung zu einer archetypischen Visualisierung der Landschaftswahrnehmung. Es fällt schwer, dabei nicht erneut an Caspar David Friedrichs *Mönch am Meer*, den *Wanderer über dem Nebelmeer* (1818) und andere seiner Gemälde zu denken, in denen im Vordergrund eine Rückenfigur stellvertretend für uns Betrachtende in die Weite der Landschaft schaut. Aber schon Kleist sprach in seinem erwähnten Aufsatz vom schmerzlichen Unvermögen, trotz diesem figürlichen Identifikationsangebot die Unmittelbarkeit der Naturerfahrung in der Betrachtung eines Bildes wiederzufinden: «Herrlich ist es in einer unendlichen Einsamkeit am Meeresufer, unter trübem Himmel, auf eine unbegrenzte Wasserwüste, hinauszuschauen. [...] und so ward ich selbst der

38
Ohne Titel / Untitled, 1997
2 Rundspiegel / 2 circular mirrors,
je / each 20 cm (Ø)
Aufhängung: Polyamidfaden / suspended on polyamide thread
Privatbesitz / Private collection

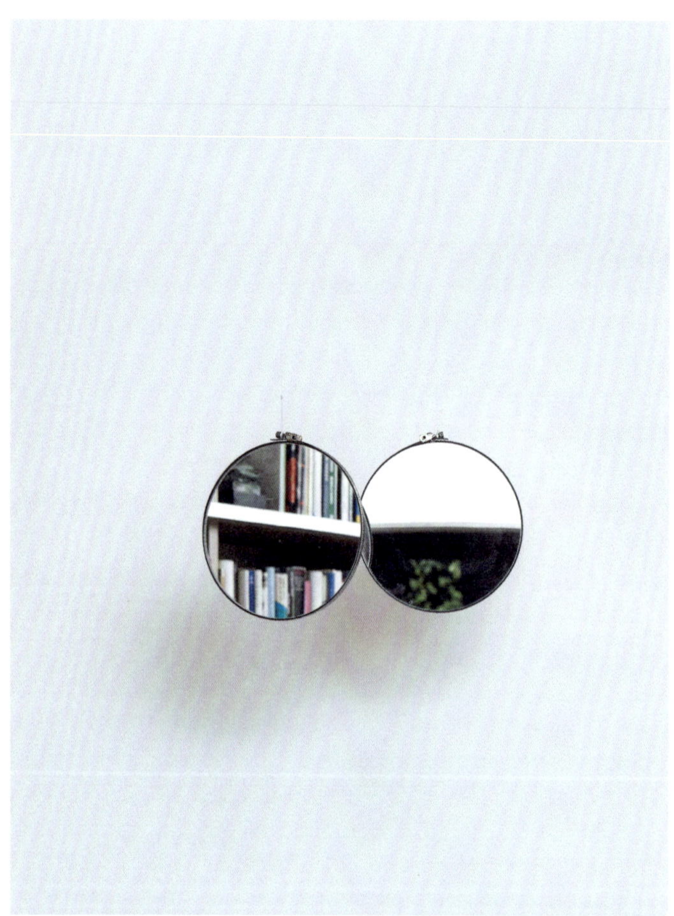

of identification, he was unable to rediscover the immediacy of the experience of nature in the contemplation of a painting: "It is a magnificent thing to look out across a boundless watery waste in infinite solitude on the seashore, under a gray sky. [...] and thus I myself became the Capuchin, the picture became the dune, but that which I should have gazed upon with longing—the sea—was altogether missing."[108] Although the elegiac atmospheric landscape is no substitute for nature, it nevertheless acts as a catalyst, prompting us to reflect on our own isolation: "Nothing could be sadder or more unnerving than this position in the world: the only spark of life in the wide realm of death, the lonely center in a lonely circle."[109] By contrast, Raetz's angularly aloof *Feldstechermann* sculptures are not mediators of an existentialist melancholy. They do not muse, but are concentrated observers of visible reality. Unlike Kleist in front of Friedrich's *Monk by the Sea*, when we gaze at the small figures as they look out

39
Das Bullauge Oder: / The Porthole Or: D'après la seconde nature, 2007–2011
Ex. / No. IV/V
Figur, oberer Teil: Birnbaumholz, gedrechselt, 16,7 cm (Höhe), unterer Teil: Birkensperrholz, verleimt, schwarz gebeizt und gewachst, 18,7 cm (Höhe), Gehäuse: Okoumé-Sperrholz, bemalt (Acrylfarbe), Front: Aluminiumblech, aufgeraut, lackiert (Zaponlack-Spray), Innenseite der Abdeckung, bemalt (blaue Kunstharzfarbe), Prospekt: Aluminiumblech, verformt; Elektromotor, 2 Leuchtstoffröhren, 155×89,6×24,5 cm (Gesamtmass) / Figure, upper part: pearwood, turned, 16,7 cm (height), lower part: birch plywood, glued, stained black and waxed, 18,7 cm (height), housing: Okoumé plywood, painted (acrylic), front, sheet aluminum, sanded, varnished (Zaponlack spray), inside of the cover, painted (blue synthetic resin), view: sheet aluminum, deformed; electric motor, 2 fluorescent tubes, 155×89,6×24,5 cm (overall dimensions)
Kunstmuseum Bern, Bern

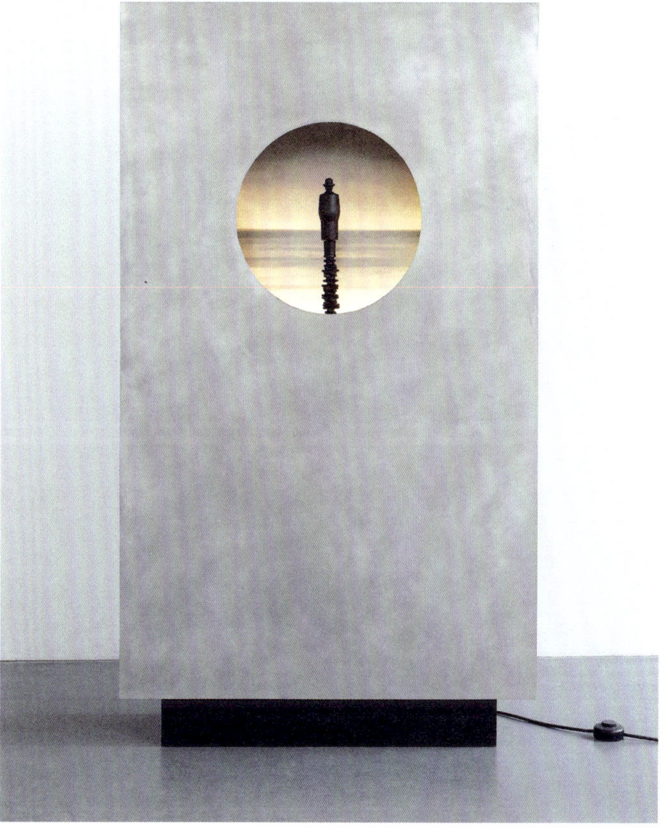

Kapuziner, das Bild ward die Düne, das aber, wo hinaus ich mit Sehnsucht blicken sollte, die See, fehlte ganz.»[108] Die elegische Stimmungslandschaft ist zwar kein Naturersatz, wirkt jedoch als Katalysator für die Reflexion des eigenen isolierten Standorts in der Welt: «Nichts kann trauriger und unbehaglicher sein, als diese Stellung in der Welt: der einzige Lebensfunke im weiten Reich des Todes, der einsame Mittelpunkt im einsamen Kreis.»[109] Raetz' kantig spröde *Feldstechermänner* hingegen sind nicht Vermittler einer existenzialistischen Melancholie, sie sinnieren nicht, sie sind konzentrierte Beobachter der sichtbaren Realität. Indem wir die kleinen Skulpturen in den Blick nehmen, wie sie an unserer Stelle über das Meer blicken, denken wir anders als Kleist angesichts von Friedrichs *Mönch am Meer* nicht über die unüberbrückbare Kluft zwischen Ich und Welt nach. Wir scheinen uns vielmehr selbst beim Schauen zuzuschauen und denken über den Unterschied zwischen der Wirklichkeit und ihrer bildlichen Erschei-

over the sea in our place, we do not reflect on the unbridgeable chasm between us and world. Instead, we seem to be looking at ourselves in the act of looking, and think about the difference between reality and its visual appearance. We are supported in this by the overall layout, almost like an experimental set-up. The vertical sculpture, the horizontal painting-like relief opposite it, and the in some cases large distance between them, spanning an entire gallery or even several rooms, represent the three elements that make up the process of seeing: the person looking, the space, and the image perceived (fig. 37). They correspond to the three axes of a spatial coordinate system.

A *Feldstechermann* entered the collection of the Aargauer Kunsthaus, too, at the same time as *Zeemansblik* number 11. The version in question is number 3/6 of the 1994 edition in cast iron.[110] This edition was based on a small edition cast in brass that same year,[111] itself modeled on a 1987 pearwood sculpture representing number 9 in the *Felderstechermann* group.[112] Raetz named the cast-metal editions *Fernseh* and *Fernsicht*, to distinguish them from the one-off versions. He found inspiration for the title *Fernsicht*, which might be translated as "distant view," in texts by the Art Brut artist Adolf Wölfli. There the term appears in descriptions of fantastical world landscapes, over which the narrator allows his eyes to rove from hot-air balloons and mountain peaks.[113] Raetz took up this motif with the small figures standing on pieces of rock. In 1997, four *Felderstechermann* versions appeared under the name *Fernsicht* in the alpine context of the exhibition *Die Schwerkraft der Berge 1774–1997.*[114] Given that these sculptures are distilled into a type and possess no specifically nautical attributes, there is nothing contradictory about their appearance in a mountainous setting. Since 1997, however, *Feldstechermann* figures have never again been combined with alpine motifs, but have only ever been presented with *Zeemansblik* reliefs or, by way of an alternative, with watercolors and prints showing the *Zeemansblik* motif. This also applies to the *Zeemansblik* and *Feldstechermann* versions in Aarau.[115]

From the end of the 1990s on, Raetz developed the work constellation further. He combined the sculptures of the figures looking through field glasses with two double-sided circular mirrors, which are suspended from the ceiling and rotate independently of each other (fig. 38). The *Zeemansblik*'s binocular field of view is here uncoupled into two individual circles. Emancipated

nung nach. Unterstützt werden wir dabei durch die geradezu modellhafte Anlage des Arrangements. Die vertikale Skulptur, das horizontale gemäldeartige Relief ihr gegenüber und die bisweilen grosse, einen ganzen Saal oder gar mehrere Räume überbrückende Distanz zwischen ihnen repräsentieren die drei für den Vorgang des Sehens konstitutiven Elemente der schauenden Person, des Raums und des wahrgenommenen Bildes (Abb. 37). Sie entsprechen den drei Achsen eines räumlichen Koordinatensystems.

Auch in die Sammlung des Aargauer Kunsthaues gelangte zusammen mit dem *Zeemansblik* ein *Feldstechermann*. Es handelt sich um das Exemplar 3/6 der 1994 ausgeführten Edition in Eisenguss[110] nach einer kleinen Auflage in Messingguss,[111] für welche die aus Birnbaumholz geschnitzte Skulptur Nr. 9 der Motivgruppe von 1987 als Modell diente.[112] Raetz nannte die Auflagen in Metallguss zur Unterscheidung von den skulptierten Vorbildern *Fernseh* und *Fernsicht*. Eine Anregung für den Titel *Fernsicht* fand er in Texten des Art-Brut-Künstlers Adolf Wölfli. Dort erscheint der Begriff in Beschreibungen fantastischer Weltlandschaften, über die der Erzähler seinen Blick von Ballonen und Berggipfeln aus schweifen lässt.[113] Mit den auf Bruchsteine gesetzten Figürchen griff Raetz dieses Motiv auf. Gleich vier Fassungen des *Feldstechermanns* waren 1997 unter der Bezeichnung *Fernsicht* in den alpinen Kontext der Ausstellung *Die Schwerkraft der Berge 1774–1997* integriert.[114] Da die zum Typus abstrahierten Skulpturen keine spezifisch seemännischen Attribute besitzen, ruft ihre Platzierung in einer gebirgigen Szenerie keinen Widerspruch hervor. In der Folge bestand das Ensemble aber wieder aus einem *Feldstechermann* und einem *Zeemansblik*. Das gilt genauso für die Aarauer Werke.[115] Statt der Reliefs können auch Aquarelle und Druckgrafiken mit dem Motiv des Meereshorizonts im Fernglasblickfeld das Gegenüber der *Feldstechermänner* bilden.

Ab Ende der 1990er Jahre entwickelte Raetz die Werkkonstellation weiter. Er kombinierte die Skulpturen der blickenden Figuren mit zwei doppelseitigen, von der Decke hängenden Rundspiegeln, die sich unabhängig voneinander drehen (Abb. 38). Das binokulare Blickfeld von *Zeemansblik* ist zu zwei individuellen Sehkreisen entkoppelt. Sie haben sich von der Fixierung auf die Wand und vom starren Blick des *Feldstechermanns* emanzipiert und konfrontieren ihn statt mit einem marinen Panorama mit kaleidoskopartig wechselnden Reflexen der Umgebung und mit seinem eigenen Spiegelbild. Der Ersatz oder vielmehr die

40
Ich sehe ein Bild / I See a Picture, 1977
Leim, mit Pigment vermischt,
auf Baumwollstoff (Leintuch) /
Glue mixed with pigment on cotton
fabric (bed sheet)
ca. 250 x 169 cm
Privatbesitz / Private collection

from a fixed position on the wall and from the *Feldstechermann*'s unwavering stare, they confront him not with a marine panorama, but instead with kaleidoscopically changing reflections of the surroundings and with his own mirror image. The replacement of *Zeemansblik*, or more accurately its dynamic modulation, did not change the fundamental theme of the ensemble: the representability of seeing. In *Das Bullauge Oder: D'après la seconde nature* (2007–2011), for example, an object resembling a peep box shows a comparable constellation of a figure standing in front of a sea view. The sculpture inside the box rotates, and in so doing generates moving reflections, while the landscape background remains static (fig. 39).[116] From the early 1990s onwards, kinetics became a fundamental design principle in Raetz's three-dimensional work. In a changed form, *Zeemansblik* also remained relevant and topical during this phase of his œuvre.

"Ich sehe ein Bild" and "Das Wetter zum Selbermachen": The Role of the Viewer in the Creation of Images

Markus Raetz's engagement with the subject of seeing translated itself into a corresponding iconography, which includes the *Zeemansblik* binocular field of view as well as the complementary *Feldstechermann* figure looking through the optical device of field glasses. But visual perception is present in Raetz's work in a broader sense, too, and is thereby inextricably linked with questions about the nature of the image and imagery. Into the middle of a large 1977 painting on cloth, he introduced the four words "ICH" "SEHE" "EIN" "BILD" ("I," "SEE," "A," "PICTURE") (fig. 40), spaced out across the entire width of the fabric support.[117] The short words, written in capital letters, are each afforded their own space and potency by the lengthy gaps between them—as if, despite their modest size, they needed to be declaimed rather than read. Top left and bottom right, as if bracketing the landscape elements and striding figures represented via illusionistic means, Raetz respectively placed pictograms of a drawing hand and a gazing head with a key for an eye. Their easily understandable symbolism lends the simple sentence the character of a manifesto. For Raetz, seeing was synonymous with the perception of images. Even his fully three-dimensional sculptures viewable from all sides of the early 1990s—whose "real subject," according to the artist, lay in their silhouettes—he regarded as

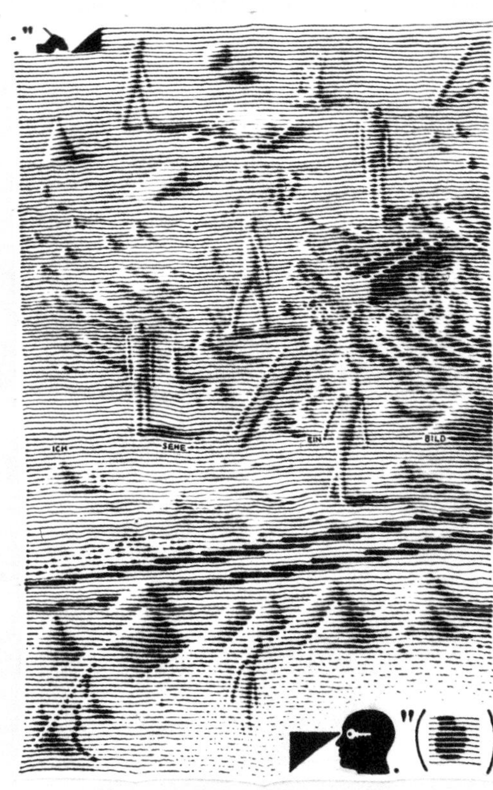

Dynamisierung von *Zeemansblik* änderte nichts an der grundlegenden Thematik des Ensembles: die Darstellbarkeit des Sehens. So dreht sich bei *Das Bullauge oder: D'après la seconde nature* (2007–2011), einem guckkastenartigen Objekt mit einer vergleichbaren Konstellation aus einer stehenden Figur vor einem Meeresprospekt, die Skulptur und ruft damit bewegte Reflexe hervor, während der landschaftliche Hintergrund statisch bleibt (Abb. 39).[116] Kinetik wurde ab den beginnenden 1990er Jahren zum fundamentalen Gestaltungsprinzip im dreidimensionalen Schaffen von Raetz. In verwandelter Form blieb *Zeemansblik* auch in dieser Werkphase relevant und aktuell.

«Ich sehe ein Bild» und «Das Wetter zum Selbermachen»: die Rolle der Betrachtenden bei der Entstehung von Bildern

Markus Raetz' Beschäftigung mit dem Thema des Sehens schlug sich in einer entsprechenden Ikonografie nieder, zu der das binokulare Blickfeld von *Zeemansblik* ebenso gehört wie die komplementäre, durch das optische Gerät des Fernglases schauende Figur des *Feldstechermanns*. Visuelle Wahrnehmung ist in seinem Werk aber in einem umfassenderen Sinn präsent und dabei unlösbar mit Fragen zum Wesen des Bildes und der Bildlichkeit verknüpft. Mitten auf ein grosses

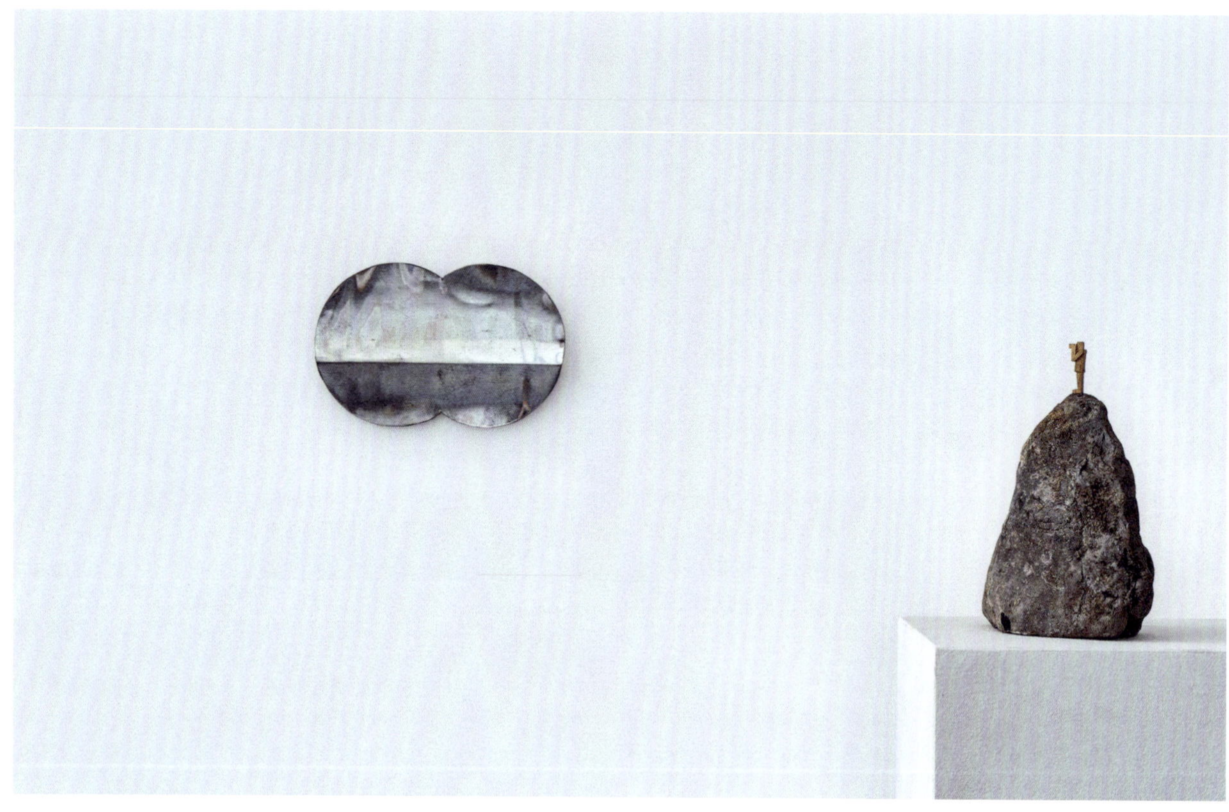

"a reservoir of two-dimensional forms".[118] His work always had its starting point in the line or the "two-dimensional retinal image."[119] Art journalist Max Wechsler described Raetz's work as a translation of "world reality" into an "image reality."[120] Like Magritte's famous epigram "Ceci n'est pas une pipe," Raetz's equally apodictic "Ich sehe ein Bild" seems to heighten awareness of the difference between reality and its image. By not referring at all to the real-life original on which his pictorial motif is based, however, and by concentrating instead on the image and the process of its perception, Raetz shifts the focus to the relationship between the image and its constitutive elements. In the case of his painting on cloth, raster-like lines, which swell and subside, fuse together in our eye into a recognizable image.

The image is not something given in advance, but something that we imagine, inspired by abstract elements such as points, lines, planes, and colors. "Perception and imagination cannot be separated," wrote Bernd Hüppauf and Christoph Wulf. "Imagination transfers into the image what is absent in the variety of data provided by sensory stimuli, and completes the only ever partially

41
Was er sieht / What He Sees, 1988
Buchenholz, geschnitzt, Kalkstein / Beech, carved, limestone,
13×6×10 cm
Weissblech (Kaffeedose), gefalzt / Tinplate (coffee tin), folded
8,5×13 cm
Privatbesitz / Private collection

sogenanntes Bildtuch von 1977 setzte er über die gesamte Breite hinweg die vier Wörter «ICH» «SEHE» «EIN» «BILD» (Abb. 40).[117] Die langen Abstände gewähren jedem der in Versalien geschriebenen, kurzen Wörter einen grossen Wirkungsraum, so als müssten sie trotz ihrer bescheidenen Dimension weniger gelesen als deklamiert werden. Gleichsam als Klammer um die illusionistisch dargestellten landschaftlichen Elemente und schreitenden Figuren platzierte Raetz oben links und unten rechts Piktogramme einer zeichnenden Hand und eines blickenden Kopfes, in dem ein Schlüssel das Auge ersetzt. Ihre leicht verständliche Symbolik verleiht dem simplen Satz den Charakter eines Manifests. Für Raetz war Sehen schlechthin gleichbedeutend mit dem Wahrnehmen von Bildern. Selbst seine vollplastischen und allansichtigen Skulpturen der frühen 1990er Jahre, deren «eigentliches Thema» ihm zufolge in ihren Silhouetten liege, betrachtete er als «ein Reservoir an zweidimensionalen Formen».[118] Der Ausgangspunkt seiner Arbeit sei immer die Linie oder das «zweidimensionale Netzhautbild» gewesen.[119] Der Kunstpublizist Max Wechsler beschrieb Raetz' Werk denn auch als eine Übersetzung der «Welt-Wirklichkeit» in eine «Bild-Wirklichkeit».[120] Wie Magrittes berühmtes Epigramm «Ceci n'est pas une pipe» scheint Raetz' ebenso apodiktischer Satz die Differenz zwischen der Wirklichkeit und ihrem Abbild ins Bewusstsein zu rücken. Indem er aber gar nicht auf das reale Vorbild des abgebildeten Motivs verweist, sondern sich auf das Bild und den Vorgang seiner Wahrnehmung konzentriert, verschiebt er den Fokus auf das Verhältnis zwischen dem Bild und seinen konstitutiven Elementen. Im Fall des genannten Bildtuchs sind es rasterartige, an- und abschwellende Linien, die sich in unserem Auge zu einem erkennbaren Bild fügen.

Das Bild ist nicht etwas vornherein Gegebenes, sondern etwas, das wir uns, angeregt durch abstrakte Elemente – Punkte, Linien, Flächen, Farben –, vorstellen. «Wahrnehmen lässt sich vom Imaginieren nicht trennen», schrieben Bernd Hüppauf und Christoph Wulf. «Die Imagination versetzt ins Bild, was in der Datenvielfalt der Sinnenreize abwesend ist und ergänzt das stets nur partiell gegebene Bild zu einem Ganzen – ohne eine kreative Einbildungskraft kein sinnvolles und zusammenhängendes Bild.»[121] Zuvor war schon Ernst Gombrich in seinem Buch *Kunst und Illusion* zu einer ähnlichen Erkenntnis gelangt: «Jedes Bild ist der Natur der Sache nach ein Appell an unsere visuelle Vorstellungskraft, und kein Bild kann ohne Ergänzung von Seiten des Beschauers verstanden

given image to make a whole—without a creative power of imagination, no meaningful and coherent image."[121] Ernst Gombrich had previously come to a similar conclusion in his book *Art and Illusion*: "Any picture, by its very nature, remains an appeal to the visual imagination; it must be supplemented in order to be understood."[122] For Gombrich, to understand a picture means to engage in an illusion, which he also called "guided projection."[123] Western art has developed various methods by which to guide projection, including perspective as the "most important trick in the armory of illusionist art," and the suggestion of light and shade, which offers "a means of vastly reducing the ambiguity of shapes as seen from one side."[124] Both illusionistic pictorial modes play a decisive role in the case of *Zeemansblik* and its effect. We might thereby speak of a reverse *trompe-l'œil*, because in place of a picture simulating three-dimensional depth, we are confronted with a three-dimensional object

42
Aus der Serie *Im Bereich des Möglichen* / From the series *In the Realm of the Possible*, 1976
Verdünnte Tinte auf Papier / Diluted ink on paper, 17×23,5 cm
Aargauer Kunsthaus, Aarau

werden.»[122] Ein Bild zu verstehen, heisst für Gombrich, sich auf eine Illusion einzulassen, die er auch «gelenkte Projektion» nannte.[123] Die westliche Kunst hat verschiedene Methoden zur Lenkung der Projektion entwickelt, beispielsweise die perspektivische Darstellung als das «wichtigste Requisit im Zauberkasten der illusionistischen Kunst» und die Andeutung von Licht und Schatten, die es ermöglicht, «die Mehrdeutigkeit, die der Darstellung von Figuren von einer einzigen Seite innewohnt, auf ein Mindestmass herabzudrücken».[124] Beide illusionistischen Bildmodi spielen für die Wirkung von *Zeemansblik* eine entscheidende Rolle. Man könnte dabei von einem umgekehrten Trompe-l'œil sprechen, denn statt mit der fingierten Dreidimensionalität eines Bildes sind wir mit der vorgetäuschten Bildlichkeit eines räumlichen Objekts konfrontiert. Erreicht wird die Illusion durch die Inversion von konkav und konvex. Die Linie des in unerreichbarer Distanz liegenden Horizonts ragt uns paradoxerweise als Falz im Blech entgegen, als wäre sie eine ironische Illustration von Walter Benjamins vielzitierter, gleichsam allzu wörtlich genommener Definition der Aura von «natürlichen Gegenständen», etwa einem Gebirgszug am Horizont, als «einmalige Erscheinung einer Ferne so nah sie sein mag».[125]

Gombrich zufolge streben wir bei der Betrachtung von illusionistischen Bildern «eine in sich widerspruchsfreie Deutung» an.[126] Das Gelingen der Illusion hängt dabei von der Situation ab, in der ein Bild wahrgenommen wird. Für *Zeemansblik* ist der Ausstellungsraum das passende Ambiente, weil wir gewohnt sind, dort an der Wand hängende Objekte als Bilder zu betrachten und entsprechend zu deuten. Unterstützt wird die Illusion durch den *Feldstechermann*, der uns als «Regisseur» in die Rolle von Betrachtenden einweist. «Was er sieht» schrieb Raetz auf die Rückseite einer zu einem *Feldstechermann* gehörenden kleinen *Zeemansblik*-Fassung (Abb. 41).[127] Auch die Fernglasblickfeld-Silhouette des Reliefs trägt zu der von Gombrich als Ziel der Illusion postulierten Eindeutigkeit der Interpretation bei. Im Gegensatz dazu ist für Gottfried Boehm «Unbestimmtheit» eine generelle Eigenschaft von Bildern, unabhängig von der Schärfe der Darstellung.[128] Je unbestimmter die Gestaltungselemente eines Werks seien, desto grösser werde der «Spielraum für das Auge». Unbestimmtheit ist seines Erachtens unverzichtbar, weil erst sie «das Faktische in die Lage versetz[t], Sich zu zeigen und Etwas zu zeigen».[129] Auf *Zeemansblik* bezogen würde das heissen, dass das als malerische Unschärfe erscheinende Schimmern der Oberfläche sowohl die

feigning to be a picture. This illusion is achieved through the inversion of concave and convex. Paradoxically, the line of the horizon lying at an unattainable distance protrudes towards us as a fold in the sheet metal, as if it were an ironic, all-too-literal illustration of Walter Benjamin's oft-quoted definition of the aura of natural objects, such as a mountain range on the horizon, as the "unique phenomenon of a distance, however close as it may be."[125]

According to Gombrich, when looking at illusionistic images, we "test [them] for coherent meaning, crystallizing [them] into shape when a consistent interpretation has been found."[126] Whether or not the illusion will succeed depends on the situation in which a picture is perceived. The exhibition space is the fitting setting for *Zeemansblik*, because we are used to reading objects hanging on gallery walls as pictures and interpreting them accordingly. The illusion is supported by the *Feldstechermann* (fig. 41), who, as "director," casts us in the role of viewer. "What he sees," wrote Raetz on the back of a small *Zeemansblik* belonging to a *Feldstechermann*.[127] The relief's binoclar-field-of-view silhouette also contributes to the coherent interpretation postulated by Gombrich as the aim of the illusion. For Gottfried Boehm, by contrast, indeterminacy is a general property of images, regardless of the sharpness of the representation.[128] The more indeterminate the design elements of a work, the greater the freedom of scope for the eye. In his opinion, indeterminacy is indispensable because it is what enables the material support "to show itself and to show something."[129] With regard to *Zeemansblik*, this would mean that the shimmering of its surface—which gives the appearance of painterly soft focus—both reveals the materiality of the sheet metal and demands that the relief is read as a seascape. In principle, these two ways of seeing do not contradict each other. The coherency of the interpretation and the indeterminacy of the design have their common denominator in the "phenomenon of the visual oscillation" of the work (Boehm) and the switching by the viewer from one reading to another (Gombrich).[130] The prerequisite for this is the reduction of the pictorial means to the barest essentials, which Markus Raetz once called "minimal realism."[131]

The title *Im Bereich des Möglichen* (*In the Realm of the Possible*) for a 1976 series of drawings in diluted ink stands programmatically for the indeterminacy in appearance that leads to an increase in "iconic potentiality."[132] With

Materialität des Blechs offenlegt als auch die Deutung des Reliefs als Marinebild einfordert. Die beiden Sichtweisen widersprechen sich nicht prinzipiell. Der gemeinsame Nenner der Eindeutigkeit der Interpretation und der Unbestimmtheit der Gestaltung liegt im «Phänomen der visuellen Oszillation» des Werks (Boehm) bzw. dem Oszillieren der Betrachtung zwischen verschiedenen «Lesarten» (Gombrich).[130] Voraussetzung dafür ist die Reduktion der bildnerischen Mittel auf das absolut Notwendige, die Markus Raetz einmal «Minimalrealismus» nannte.[131]

Der Titel *Im Bereich des Möglichen* für eine Serie von Zeichnungen aus verdünnter Tinte von 1976 steht programmatisch für die Unbestimmtheit in der Erscheinung, die zur Steigerung der «ikonischen Potenzialität» führt.[132] Mit ihren weich verfliessenden hellen und dunklen Partien sind es sozusagen Bilder im Konjunktiv, denen wir die Bestimmung von Landschaften im Gegenglicht geben (Abb. 42). Für Raetz gehörten die Blätter zur Genealogie von *Zeemansblik*. Wegen seiner auf grösstmögliche Suggestivität ausgerichteten Ökonomie und Präzision im Einsatz der gestalterischen Mittel – hier beispielsweise Flecken, angeregt von Alexander Cozens Blotting-Verfahren – nannte Bernhard Bürgi ihn einen «Akrobat auf dem Nullpunkt der bildnerischen Tätigkeit».[133] Mit Blick auf das nicht gemalte Bild von *Zeemansblik* trifft die Formulierung in besonderem Mass zu. Wie die Strukturen in Marmor oder in Achaten, die im 17. und 18. Jahrhundert als Darstellungen von Landschaften, insbesondere von Meer und Wolken, genutzt wurden, zählt die blecherne Marine zu den von Jurgis Baltrušaitis als «imaginäre Realitäten» bezeichneten Erscheinungen.[134] Oder vielmehr befähigte Raetz durch seine so minimalen wie präzisen gestalterischen Eingriffe «ein lächerliches Stück Blech, ein Nichts an Bedeutung»[135], eine Realität zu enthüllen, die vorher nicht existiert hatte.

Die Feststellung, ein Bild zu sehen, bezieht sich nicht nur auf das betreffende Bild und auf andere Artefakte, die von vornherein als Bilder beabsichtigt waren. Sie greift aus auf Bilder, die in Formen und Strukturen lediglich latent vorhanden sind. Dario Gamboni bezeichnete sie als «potential images», die in der Moderne eine besondere Rolle spielen.[136] Horst Bredekamp wies in seiner *Theorie des Bildakts* ebenfalls darauf hin, dass ein Weg von Cozens *blots* «in die Moderne und deren Faible für die Eigenmotorik der abstrakten Form» führt.[137] Sein Buch widmete er «den Zufallsbildern der Wolkengebirge».[138] Wie er war Raetz fasziniert

43
Erste Ausführung der Installation *Ohne Titel (Wolke)* / First presentation of the installation *Untitled (Cloud)*, ca. 30 Drahtplastiken mit Segeln aus getriebenem Aluminiumblech / ca. 30 wire sculptures with sails of sheet aluminum, Kunstmuseum Bern, 2023–2024

their softly flowing areas of light and dark, they are, so to speak, pictures in the subjunctive, which we determine to be landscapes seen against the light (fig. 42). For Raetz, the sheets belonged to the genealogy of *Zeemansblik*. The economy and precision with which he deployed his creative means—here, for example, blotches, inspired by Alexander Cozen's blotting process—led Bernhard Bürgi to describe Raetz as an "acrobat at the zero point of artistic activity."[133] This description is particularly fitting when we consider the non-painted image conjured by *Zeemansblik*. Like the structures in marble or agate used in the seventeenth and eighteenth centuries as representations of landscapes, in particular of sea and clouds, the sheet-metal seascape is one of the phenomena described by Jurgis Baltrušaitis as "imaginary realities."[134] Through his minimal and precise creative interventions, Raetz enabled "a trivial, utterly insignificant piece of tin"[135] to reveal a reality that had not existed before.

The conclusion that we are seeing a picture is founded not only on the picture concerned and on other artefacts that were intended as pictures from the outset, but draws more widely upon images that are merely latently present in shapes and structures. Dario Gamboni describes these as "potential images" and considers that they play a particular role in modern art.[136] Horst Bredekamp, in his *Theorie des Bildakts*, likewise identified a path leading from Cozen's blots "into modernism and its predilection for the intrinsic motor functions of the abstract form."[137] He dedicated his book to "the chance images in banks of cloud."[138] Raetz, too, was fascinated by pareidolia: that is, the seeing of figures and faces in objects and above all in phenomena of nature. Perceiving the omnipresence of images not made by human hand requires the readiness to read these into the visible world.

In the sentence "I see a picture," the subject seems to be the artist, its author. It switches to the viewer, however, because the verb is about the act of seeing. It is the person looking who, analogous to reading the sentence, allows the components perceived on the pictorial plane to form a coherent image in the true sense. In black on white in *Ich sehe ein Bild*, Raetz documented the need for the viewer's participation in order for a picture to take shape, and moreover summarized the conviction that we only see when we see a picture. Conversely, a picture in the conventional sense, as embodied by a seascape, is always a paradigmatic representation of seeing.

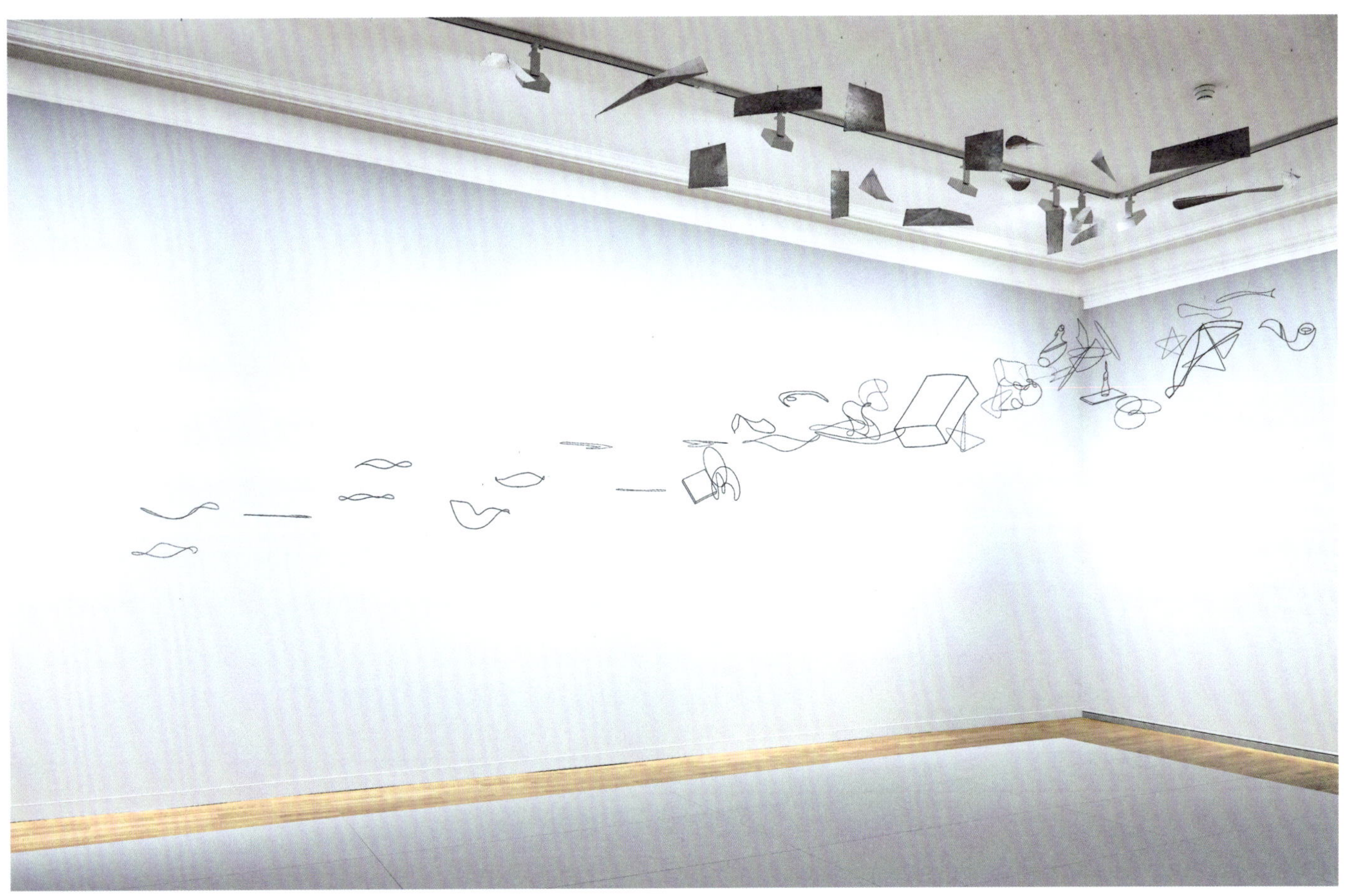

von der Pareidolie, dem Phänomen, in Gegenständen und vor allem in Erscheinungen der Natur Gestalten und Gesichter zu entdecken. Voraussetzung für die Wahrnehmung der Allgegenwärtigkeit von Bildern, die nicht von Menschenhand gemacht sind, ist die Bereitschaft, sie in die sichtbare Welt hineinzusehen.

Das Subjekt im Satz «Ich sehe ein Bild» scheint identisch mit dem Künstler, seinem Autor. Es wechselt aber auf die Seite der Betrachterin oder des Betrachters, denn benannt wird ja die Tätigkeit des Sehens. Die schauende Person ist es, die analog zur Lektüre des Satzes die wahrgenommenen Bestandteile auf der Fläche im eigentlichen Sinn erst zum kohärenten Bild werden lässt. Schwarz auf Weiss hielt Raetz auf dem Bildtuch die Notwendigkeit der Partizipation der Betrachterinnen und Betrachter an der Genese eines Bildes fest und fasste darüber hinaus die Überzeugung zusammen, dass wir nur sehen, wenn wir ein Bild sehen. Umgekehrt ist ein Bild im herkömmlichen Verständnis, wie es ein Marinebild verkörpert, stets eine paradigmatische Darstellung des Sehens.

For a picture, the dispositive of perception is the static viewer facing it. Sculpture, on the other hand, requires movement in space, be it on the part of the object being viewed or of the persons viewing it. We are able to perceive *Zeemansblik* as a singular, painting-like picture owing to the iconic frontality inherent in its silhouette. But as soon as we emancipate ourselves from our *Feldstechermann* double, begin moving and shift our point of view, it reveals itself as a sculptural object. As the angle from which we look alters, so the reflections on the sheet metal change, and in passing by we activate a stream of images of weather, as if we were starting a time-lapse film. In January 1985, in the immediate run-up to the *Zeemansblik* series, Raetz created an object consisting of a box with a folded sheet of paper, featuring a very rudimentary painting of the sea, sky, and a cliff, mounted inside it. On the back of the box, he wrote "NEU. DAS WETTER ZUM SELBERMACHEN" (NEW. DIY WEATHER) and thereby pointed laconically to the purpose of this unpretentious work and of *Zeemansblik*.[139] Even if irony is at play here, the weather is a fitting metaphor for Raetz's understanding of the image as a transitory phenomenon, which we ourselves help to make visible by seeing it.

Zeemansblik marks an important stage in Markus Raetz's œuvre. The work forms the vanishing point of an entire universe of motifs. The genre of landscape subsequently played almost no role in his sculptural œuvre, and the majority, too, of his visual metaphors for seeing, such as the eye, the field of view, and the cone of vision, reappeared only sporadically in his later work. Visual perception as the seeing of images nevertheless remained Raetz's fundamental theme. It finds expression in sculptural anamorphoses and metamorphoses with other motifs. Gamboni called these "meta-images," since they "constitute both reflections on and demonstrations of perception."[140] For these works, space and movement are likewise essential with regard to their appearance as images that are continuously transforming. As from the mid-1990s, Raetz turned to planar works made of sheet aluminum—following on, with this material, from *Zeemansblik*—and linear wire sculptures, which free themselves from the reference to the floor and the wall. Suspended from the ceiling and revolving, they allow us to forget their materiality (fig. 43). Like clouds, from time to time they permit us to see images in their changing shapes.

Das einem Bild entsprechende Dispositiv der Wahrnehmung ist das statische Vis-à-vis. Skulptur verlangt hingegen die Bewegung, sei es die des betrachteten Objekts oder sei es diejenige der Personen im Raum, die das Werk betrachten. Die in seiner Silhouette angelegte ikonische Frontalität lässt uns *Zeemansblik* als ein singuläres gemäldeartiges Bild wahrnehmen. Sobald wir uns aber von unserem Double des *Feldstechermanns* emanzipieren, uns in Bewegung setzen und unseren Blickpunkt verschieben, offenbart es sich als skulpturales Objekt. Mit unserem Perspektivenwechsel verändern sich die Reflexe auf dem Blech, und wir aktivieren im Vorbeigehen einen ganzen Strom von Witterungsbildern, als würden wir einen Film im Zeitraffer starten. Auf die Rückseite eines in eine Schachtel eingefügten, gefalzten Papiers mit der gemalten Andeutung von Meer, Himmel und einer Klippe, das im Januar 1985 im unmittelbaren Vorfeld der *Zeemansblik*-Serie entstand, verwies Ratz lakonisch auf den Zweck der unprätentiösen Arbeit und von *Zeemansblik*: «NEU. DAS WETTER ZUM SELBERMACHEN».[139] Auch wenn hier Ironie im Spiel ist, das Wetter ist eine passende Metapher für Raetz' Verständnis des Bildes als transitorisches Phänomen, dem wir selbst zur Sichtbarkeit verhelfen, indem wir es sehen.

Zeemansblik markiert eine wichtige Etappe im Schaffen von Markus Raetz. Das Werk bildet den Fluchtpunkt eines ganzen motivischen Universums. Das Genre der Landschaft spielte in der Folge kaum mehr eine Rolle im skulpturalen Œuvre und auch die meisten Bildmetaphern für das Sehen wie das Auge, das Blickfeld und der Sehkegel erscheinen später nur noch sporadisch. Visuelle Wahrnehmung als Sehen von Bildern bleibt aber weiterhin die grundlegende Thematik. Zum Ausdruck kommt sie in plastischen Anamorphosen und Metamorphosen mit anderen Motiven. Gamboni nannte sie Meta-Bilder, da sie die Wahrnehmung und ihre Reflexion zusammenführen.[140] Für sie sind der Raum und die Bewegung ebenfalls essenziell hinsichtlich ihrer Erscheinung als Bilder, die sich kontinuierlich verwandeln. Ab Mitte der 1990er Jahre wandte sich Raetz flächigen Arbeiten aus Aluminiumblech – die mit diesem Werkstoff an *Zeemansblik* anschliessen – und linearen Plastiken aus Draht zu, die sich vom Bezug zum Boden und zur Wand lösen. Von der Decke hängend und sich drehend, lassen sie ihre Materialität vergessen (Abb. 43). Wie Wolken erlauben sie uns, im Wandel ihrer Gestalt von Zeit zu Zeit Bilder zu sehen.

Notes

1 Dieter Koepplin, press release dated July 28, 1989, for the exhibition *Markus Raetz. Installation, Zeichnungen*, Museum für Gegenwartskunst, Basel, July 29 to September 25, 1989.

2 On the *Zeemansblik* work group, see Franz Müller, *Markus Raetz. Das plastische Werk. Catalogue raisonné*, with contributions by Katharina Ammann, Andrea Arnold, and Patricia Bieder, Zurich: Schweizerisches Institut für Kunstwissenschaft / Scheidegger & Spiess, 2023 (Œuvrekataloge Schweizer Künstler und Künstlerinnen 30), pp. 209–213; nos. 530–548.

3 Biography, comprehensive bibliography, and complete list of exhibitions, ibid.

4 *Blickwechsel. Texte zum Werk von Markus Raetz*, ed. Stephan Kunz, Aarau: Aargauer Kunsthaus / Nuremberg: Verlag für modern Kunst, 2005.

5 Müller 2023 (as note 2), nos. 547, 541.

6 Ibid., nos. 533, 546.

7 "Freundorfer" cliché plates with backs in most cases painted red.

8 Rainer Michael Mason, *Markus Raetz. Die Druckgraphik. Les Estampes. The Prints. Catalogue raisonné 1951–2013*, Zurich: Scheidegger & Spiess, 2014, no. 233.

9 Müller 2023 (as note 2), no. 547.

10 Delivery note from the company Kiener und Wittlin AG, Bern, preserved in the estate of Markus Raetz, Bern. Titanium zinc from the manufacturer Rheinzink is an alloy of 99.995% pure primary zinc with very small quantities of copper and titanium.

11 No. 12: Müller 2023 (as note 2), no. 542, since 1990 Museum of Contemporary Art San Diego, La Jolla; no. 11, ibid., no. 541, since 2000 Aargauer Kunsthaus, Aarau.

12 The relief is dated "MÄRZ 1987" ("MARCH 1987") in two places on the back, namely top left and top center, on the thin battens of wood attached in January 1988 as a wall mount. The metal sheet is 1 mm thick.

13 Of the seventeen versions numbered by Raetz, only no. 3 (Müller 2023 [as note 2], no. 532) exhibits slightly different proportions to the rest. These are of almost no visual consequence, however. In Müller 2023 (as note 2), no. 546, which falls outside the series, the two circular discs are positioned in such a way that their area of intersection is smaller than in the other *Zeemansblik* versions.

14 Shortly before creating the first *Zeemansblik*, on July 9, 1985, Raetz produced a small version with circular discs of different sizes. The sheet metal is painted in oil in a shade of light blue, whereby the brushstroke imitates the waves of the sea and the clouds. Raetz gave this work, which differs formally from the *Zeemansblik* series, two title variants: *Schräger Blick* (Oblique View) and *Die Gitarre UND das Meer* (The Guitar AND the Sea). The first variant suggests a perspective distortion of the motif, while the second cites Freddy Quinn's 1959 hit song of the same name and interweaves the binocular view of the sea with the shape of the soundbox of a guitar (handwritten note by Markus Raetz, Estate of Markus Raetz, Bern). Raetz did not pursue this variant any further.

15 Mason 2014 (as note 8), nos. 322, 323, dated 2001. The above-mentioned drypoint etching *Sehfeld* of 1986 (ibid., no. 233) adopts the *Zeemansblik* form in the shape of the printing plate, but not its motif.

16 *Zeemansblik* no. 12 (Müller 2023 [as note 2], no. 542) was shown in Venice.

17 François Grundbacher, "Der Gegen-Stand der Dinge" / "The Op-Posite of Things", in: *Parkett*, 8, 1986, pp. 55–65 (German), pp. 61–64 (English). The full-page illustrations appear at the start of the volume on pages 1, 3, and 4.

18 *Rücksicht. 40 Jahre Kunst in der Schweiz*, eds. Beat Wismer and Stephan Kunz, Aarau: Aargauer Kunsthaus, 2000. The work is reproduced again on p. 281.

19 Max Matter, *Sehsea*, 1995, digital transfer process, 50 × 70 cm; Michel Grillet, *Die Farbschachtel von dem Aargauer Kunsthaus*, 2010, gouache on gouache pastilles, plastic paint box; Gaspare O. Melcher, *Hommage an Raetz*, 2013, collage on canvas, 95 × 95 cm.

20 The incorrect spelling "Szeemansblik" for version no. 1 in an article in the art journal *Kunst-Bulletin* could be interpreted as an unintentional homage to the Bern Kunsthalle director and curator Harald Szeemann (1933–2005), who was important for the early years of Raetz's artistic career (Max Wechsler, "Markus Raetz. Vom Fluss der Figurationen zwischen den Figuren," in: *Das Kunst-Bulletin*, 1994, 4, pp. 12–19, caption p. 14).

21 Müller 2023 (as note 2), nos. 568.1–568.16, 570.

22 Homophones: *Schema* (ibid., no. 151), *J'aime A* (no. 157), *Warum nicht Niesen* (no. 359), *Niesen bitte!* (no. 360), *Des Seins* (no. 691); homographs: *Schiefer Schiefer* (no. 1018); anagrams: *Flas und Glasche* (no. 606) and *Die falschen Flaschen* (no. 607).

23 *Markus Raetz. Le reflet des mots*, Montricher: Fondation Jan Michalski, March 18 to July 10, 2022 (exhibition and catalog by Rainer Michael Mason).

24 Müller 2023 (as note 2), no. 807.

25 Helen Lagger, "'Ich sehe auch in Holzmaserungen Gestalten,'" in: *Berner Zeitung*, February 10, 2014, pp. 10–11, quote p. 10: "Mit Zeichnen kann man etwas Ähnliches machen wie mit Schrift, nämlich einen Charakter beschreiben. Die Profile sind für mich fast wie Buchstaben."

26 Müller 2023 (as note 2), no. 1138.

27 Ibid., no. 940.

28 *Wasser für den Mars*, ibid., no. 126. Translator's note: *Wasser für den Mars* is the title under which Asimov's 1952 novella *The Martian Way* was published in German.

29 Michel Butor, *Boomerang*, Paris: Gallimard, 1978. Müller 2023 (as note 2), nos. 411–423.

30 Müller 2023 (as note 2), no. 937. Ali spontaneously declaimed "Me – We" during a speech on July 4, 1975, at Harvard, when he was asked by the audience to recite a poem. According to an alternative tradition, the poem instead ran "Me? Whee!".

31 Mason 2014 (as note 8), no. 327.

32 Müller 2023 (as note 2), nos. 935–936.

33 Ibid., nos. 709–712.

34 *Impressions d'impressions d'Afrique*, Mason 2014 (as note 8), nos. 175–190. Raymond Roussel, *Eindrücke aus Afrika*, Munich: Matthes & Seitz, 1980.

35 Müller 2023 (as note 2), nos. 375, 631–634.

36 Arturo Schwarz, *The Complete Works of Marcel Duchamp. Revised and Expanded Edition*, London: Thames & Hudson, 1997, no. 391.

37 Müller 2023 (as note 2), no. 359.

38 *René Magritte. Catalogue raisonné*, ed. David Sylvester, Basel: Wiese Verlag, 1992–1997, vol. 3 (1993), no. 1013. The full title of Raetz's furniture-like kinetic sculpture is *Das Bullauge*

Anmerkungen

1 Dieter Koepplin, auf 28.7.1989 datierter Pressetext zur Ausstellung *Markus Raetz. Installation, Zeichnungen*, Museum für Gegenwartskunst, Basel, 29.7.–25.9.1989.

2 Zu dieser Werkgruppe: Franz Müller, *Markus Raetz. Das plastische Werk. Catalogue raisonné*, mit Beiträgen von Katharina Ammann, Andrea Arnold und Patricia Bieder, Zürich: Schweizerisches Institut für Kunstwissenschaft / Scheidegger & Spiess, 2023 (Œuvrekataloge Schweizer Künstler und Künstlerinnen 30), S. 209–213; Nr. 530–548.

3 Biografie sowie umfassende Bibliografie und vollständiges Ausstellungsverzeichnis bei ebd.

4 *Blickwechsel. Texte zum Werk von Markus Raetz*, hrsg. von Stephan Kunz, Aarau: Aargauer Kunsthaus / Nürnberg: Verlag für moderne Kunst, 2005.

5 Müller 2023 (wie Anm. 2), Nr. 547, Nr. 541.

6 Ebd., Nr. 533, Nr. 546.

7 «Freundorfer» Klischeeplatten mit meist rot bemalten Rückseiten.

8 Rainer Michael Mason, *Markus Raetz. Die Druckgraphik. Les Estampes. The Prints. Catalogue raisonné 1951–2013*, Zürich: Scheidegger & Spiess, 2014, Nr. 233.

9 Müller 2023 (wie Anm. 2), Nr. 547.

10 Lieferschein der Firma Kiener und Wittlin AG, Bern, im Nachlass Markus Raetz, Bern. Beim Titanzink der Marke «Rheinzink» handelt es sich um eine Legierung aus Elektrolyt-Feinzink mit 99,995-prozentigem Reinheitsgrad und kleinsten Mengen an Kupfer und Titan.

11 Nr. 12, Müller 2023 (wie Anm. 2), Nr. 542, seit 1990 im Museum of Contemporary Art San Diego, La Jolla. Nr. 11, ebd., Nr. 541, seit 2000 im Aargauer Kunsthaus, Aarau.

12 Das Relief ist rückseitig oben links und oben in der Mitte der im Januar 1988 angebrachten, aus flachen Holzleisten gefügten Aufhängevorrichtung jeweils mit «MÄRZ 1987» datiert. Die Stärke des Blechs beträgt 1 mm.

13 Von den 17 von Raetz nummerierten Exemplaren weist lediglich Nr. 3 (Müller 2023 [wie Anm. 2], Nr. 532) leicht von den anderen Fassungen abweichende Proportionen auf, die aber optisch kaum ins Gewicht fallen. Bei Müller 2023 (wie Anm. 2), Nr. 546, das ausserhalb der Reihe figuriert, sind die beiden Kreisscheiben hingegen so angeordnet, dass sie eine kleinere Schnittfläche bilden als bei den übrigen Fassungen von *Zeemansblik*.

14 Kurz vor dem ersten Exemplar von *Zeemansblik* entstand am 9.7.1985 eine kleine Fassung mit unterschiedlich grossen Kreisscheiben. Das Blech ist mit Ölfarbe hellblau bemalt, der Pinselduktus imitiert die Wellen des Meeres und die Wolken. Dem von der folgenden Serie formal abweichenden Werk verlieh Raetz die Titelvarianten *Schräger Blick* und *Die Gitarre UND das Meer*. Die erste Variante suggeriert eine perspektivische Verzerrung des Motivs, die zweite zitiert Freddy Quinns gleichnamigen Schlager von 1959 und verschränkt den binokularen Blick auf das Meer mit der Form des Schallkörpers einer Gitarre (handschriftliche Notiz von Markus Raetz, Nachlass Markus Raetz, Bern). Raetz verfolgte diese Variante nicht weiter.

15 Mason 2014 (wie Anm. 8), Nr. 322 und 323, datiert 2001. Die oben erwähnte Kaltnadel-Radierung *Sehfeld* von 1986 (ebd., Nr. 233) übernimmt die Form von *Zeemansblik* in der Gestalt der Druckplatte, nicht jedoch das Motiv.

16 Ausgestellt war *Zeemansblik* 12 (Müller 2023 [wie Anm. 2], Nr. 542).

17 François Grundbacher, «Der Gegen-Stand der Dinge. The Op-Posite of Things», in: *Parkett*, 8, 1986, S. 55–65, englische Übersetzung S. 61–64. Die ganzseitigen Abbildungen befinden sich vor den Essays auf den Seiten 1, 3 und 4.

18 *Rücksicht. 40 Jahre Kunst in der Schweiz*, hrsg. von Beat Wismer und Stephan Kunz, Aarau: Aargauer Kunsthaus, 2000. Das Werk ist noch einmal auf S. 281 reproduziert.

19 Max Matter, *Sehsea*, 1995, digitales Transferverfahren, 50 × 70 cm; Michel Grillet, *Die Farbschachtel von dem Aargauer Kunsthaus*, 2010, Gouache auf Gouachepastillen, Farbschachtel aus Kunststoff; Gaspare O. Melcher, *Hommage an Raetz*, 2013, Collage auf Leinwand, 95 × 95 cm.

20 Die falsche Schreibweise «Szeemansblik» für die Fassung Nr. 1 in einem Artikel des *Kunst-Bulletin* könnte als unfreiwillige Reverenz an den Berner Kunsthalleleiter und Kurator Harald Szeemann (1933–2005), der für die frühen Jahre von Raetz' künstlerischem Werdegang von Bedeutung war, aufgefasst werden (Max Wechsler, «Markus Raetz. Vom Fluss der Figurationen zwischen den Figuren», in: *Das Kunst-Bulletin*, 4, 1994, S. 12–19, Abbildungslegende S. 14).

21 Müller 2023 (wie Anm. 2), Nr. 568.1–568.16, 570.

22 Homophone: *Schema* (Ebd., Nr. 151) – *J'aime A* (Nr. 157.), *Warum nicht Niesen* (Nr. 359), *Niesen bitte!* (Nr. 360), *Des Seins* (Nr. 691), Homographen: *Schiefer Schiefer* (Nr. 1018), Anagramme: *Flas und Glasche* (Nr. 606) oder *Die falschen Flaschen* (Nr. 607).

23 *Markus Raetz. Le reflet des mots*, Montricher: Fondation Jan Michalski, 18.3.–10.7.2022 (Ausstellung und Katalog von Rainer Michael Mason).

24 Müller 2023 (wie Anm. 2), Nr. 807.

25 Helen Lagger, «‹Ich sehe auch in Holzmaserungen Gestalten›», in: *Berner Zeitung*, 10.2.2014, S. 10–11, Zitat S. 10.

26 Müller 2023 (wie Anm. 2), Nr. 1138.

27 Ebd., Nr. 940.

28 *Wasser für den Mars* (ebd., Nr. 126).

29 Michel Butor, *Boomerang*, Paris: Gallimard, 1978. Müller 2023 (wie Anm. 2), Nr. 411–423.

30 Müller 2023 (wie Anm. 2), Nr. 937. Ali deklamierte «Me – We» spontan während einer Rede am 4.7.1975 in Harvard, als er aus dem Publikum zur Rezitation eines Gedichts aufgefordert wurde. Einer alternativen Überlieferung zufolge lautete das Gedicht eher «Me? Whee!».

31 Mason 2014 (wie Anm. 8), Nr. 327.

32 Müller 2023 (wie Anm. 2), Nr. 935–936.

33 Ebd., Nr. 709–712.

34 «Impressions d'impressions d'Afrique», Mason 2014 (wie Anm. 8), Nr. 175–190. Raymond Roussel, *Eindrücke aus Afrika*, München: Matthes & Seitz, 1980.

35 Müller 2023 (wie Anm. 2), Nr. 375, 631–634.

36 Arturo Schwarz, *The Complete Works of Marcel Duchamp. Revised and Expanded Edition*, London: Thames & Hudson, 1997, Nr. 391.

37 Müller 2023 (wie Anm. 2), Nr. 359.

38 *René Magritte. Catalogue raisonné*, hrsg. von David Sylvester, Basel: Wiese Verlag, 1992–1997, Band III, 1993, Nr. 1013. Raetz' möbelartige, kinetische Skulptur heisst mit vollem Titel *Das Bullauge Oder: D'après la seconde nature* (Müller 2023 [wie Anm. 2], Nr. 1037).

39 Ebd., Nr. 636–639.

40 Sylvester 1992–1997 (wie Anm. 38), Band I, 1992, Nr. 303.

41 Mason 2014 (wie Anm. 8), Nr. 243.

42 «Alles und nichts: ein Wechselspiel», Interview von Konrad Tobler mit Markus Raetz, in: *Berner Zeitung*, 13.5.1998.

43 Koepplin 1989 (wie Anm. 1).

Oder: D'après la seconde nature. See Müller 2023 (as note 2) no. 1037.

39 Müller 2023 (as note 2), nos. 636–639. *Nichtpfeife* may be translated as "non-pipe" or "not-a-pipe."

40 Sylvester 1992–1997 (as note 38), vol. 1 (1992), no. 303.

41 Mason 2014 (as note 8), no. 243.

42 "Alles und nichts: ein Wechselspiel," interview with Markus Raetz by Konrad Tobler, in: *Berner Zeitung*, May 13, 1998: "Ich denke immer wieder darüber nach, wie René Magritte die Wörter braucht."

43 Koepplin 1989 (as note 1).

44 Toni Stooss, "Einleitung. Vom Leinwandknick zum *Zeemansblik*," in: *Markus Raetz. Arbeiten 1962 bis 1986*, catalog of the exhibition at the Kunsthaus Zürich, Zurich: Edition Stähli, 1986, pp. 7–9, quote p. 7: "Auf das Werk von Markus Raetz übertragen wären durch jene Linien 'Themen' verschiedener Qualität verbunden: etwa die Anwendung einer bestimmten Technik, einer wieder aufgenommenen Struktur, eines wiederkehrenden Bildmotivs oder gar desselben Grundgedankens, der eine jeweils unterschiedliche sinnliche Formulierung erfährt."

45 Gilbert Lascault, "Notizen zu einem Raetz-Dictionnaire," in: ibid., pp. 53–61, quote p. 60: "M. R. liebt Spiralen. Über alles."

46 Müller 2023 (as note 2), no. 493.

47 *Markus Raetz: Polaroids 1978–1993*, foreword by Ad Petersen, Musée d'art et d'histoire, Geneva, 1994 (published in conjunction with the exhibition held at IVAM Centro Julio González, Valencia [October 7, 1993 to January 2, 1994], the Serpentine Gallery, London [March 16 to April 24, 1994] and the Musée Rath, Geneva [June 17 to September 11, 1994]), p. 85.

48 Ibid, p. 94.

49 Toni Stooss coined the pithy—and in German rhyming—phrase as the subtitle to his introduction to the catalog of the 1986 Raetz exhibition at the Kunsthaus Zürich (see note 44).

50 Müller 2023 (as note 2), nos. 45, 48.

51 One relief is titled *La Cacahouète* as a consequence of this visual association: see Müller 2023 (as note 2), no. 66.

52 Ibid., no. 68.

53 Jürgen Glaesemer, "Über die Zeichnungen von Markus Raetz," in: idem, *"Das Beobachten des Beobachtens," Markus Raetz. Zeichnungen*, Bern: Kunstmuseum 1977, pp. 9–30, here p. 9.

54 Raetz in an interview with Hans-Joachim Müller, in: *Prix Meret Oppenheim 2006. Gamboni, Raetz, Schelbert, Suermondt, Winnewisser, Zumthor*, Bern: Bundesamt für Kultur, 2007, pp. 25–37, quote p. 28: "In jedem Fall ist Zeichnen fast immer der erste Schritt – auch bei den Skulpturen. Was zu ihnen führt, führt über die Zeichnung."

55 Raetz in the documentary film *Markus Raetz* by Iwan Schumacher, Zurich: Schumacher & Frey, 2007; cited here from Walter Keller, "Markus Raetz: falsch betrachtet – richtig gesehen," in: *Du*, 68, 2008/9, pp. 104–111, quote p. 105. On *Eva*: Müller 2023 (as note 2), no. 226.

56 Published as a facsimile: Markus Raetz, *Die Bücher*, Zurich: Galerie und Edition Stähli, 1975, vol. 2, unpaginated.

57 Ibid., vol. 3, unpaginated. The original note reads: "Form des 'Gesichtsfeldes' als Umrissform f. Zeichnung. Auf Punkt P schauen, während mit Bleistift die Grenzlinie des Gesichtsfeldes markiert wird."

58 Ernst Mach, *Die Analyse der Empfindungen und das Verhältnis des Physischen zum Psychischen*, 2nd edition, Jena: Fischer, 1900, p. 15, fig. 1.

59 The illustration from Mach's book and Raetz's drawing are reproduced in: Glaesemer 1977 (as note 53), p. 19.

60 Mason 2014 (as note 8), no. 233, second state.

61 Müller 2023 (as note 2), no. 677.

62 Drawing of July 26, 1985, reproduced in: Gilbert Lascault, "Die Augen und das Sehen in einigen Werken von Markus Raetz" / "The Eyes, the Sight, in Some Works by Markus Raetz" / "Les Yeux, la vue, á partir de certaines œuvres de Markus Raetz," in: *Parkett*, 8, 1986, pp. 30–36 (German), pp. 38–42 (English), pp. 43–45 (French), fig. p. 31.

63 Lascault 1986a (as note 45), pp. 53–61, quote p. 54: "Hier wird alles durch approximative Ähnlichkeiten zwischen dem Betrachter und dem Betrachteten in Gang gebracht. Die Augen haben ungefähr die Form von Brüsten, der Warze entspricht in etwa [der] Augapfel. M. R. weist gewissermassen auf eine Art Grundharmonie zwischen dem Begehrenden und dem Begehrten hin."

64 Lascault 1986b (as note 62), p. 39.

65 The drawing, dated July 24/25 1985, is reproduced in: Gilbert Lascault, "Fugues et variations des lignes," in: *Markus Raetz*, catalog of the exhibition at the Carré d'Art – Musée d'art contemporain, Nîmes, Arles: Actes Sud, 2006, pp. 9–43, fig. p. 39.

66 In addition to the drawing of July 26, 1985 (see note 62), a further sheet dated July 24, 1985 featuring the mask motif is reproduced in: Lascault 1986b (as note 62), fig. p. 42.

67 Müller 2023 (as note 2), no. 344.

68 Art and violent crime are parallelized or brought very close together in Raetz's work, too. In a small painting in somber hues (Müller 2023 [as note 2], no. 484.22), two figures in rear view, each with the letter M painted on their back, and two figures lying down are arranged one beside the other. Of the first pair, one is holding a paintbrush in his raised hand, and the other a knife. The letter M on the backs of the artist and the murderer stands simultaneously for painting (in German, *Malerei*), murder, Markus, and Manet, as the two reclining male bodies are a quotation from Edouard Manet's 1864/65 painting *The Dead Toreador* (National Gallery of Art, Washington, DC). The letter M is also a reference to the 1931 German movie classic *M – Eine Stadt sucht einen Mörder* by Fritz Lang (1890–1976), or to the 1954 crime thriller movie *Dial M for Murder* by Alfred Hitchcock (1899–1980).

69 "Wölflis Formenvokabular. Gezeichnet von Markus Rätz [sic]," in: *Adolf Wölfli. Schreiber, Dichter, Zeichner, Componist*, with texts by Daniel Baumann et al.; published by the Adolf-Wölfli-Stiftung, Kunstmuseum Bern, Basel: Wiese Verlag, 1996, pp. 226–227.

70 Reproduced in: Lascault 1986b (as note 62), fig. p. 42.

71 Lagger 2014 (as note 25), p. 10: "Mir gefällt an den Cartoons vor allem die Reduktion aufs Wesentliche, die Tatsache, dass man mit wenigen Strichen etwas erzählen kann."

72 Jean-Christophe Ammann, "Fünf junge Berner Künstler: Werro, Raetz, Fivian, Gertsch, Distel," in: *Das Werk*, 55, 1968, pp. 245–250, here p. 245: "Konstituierung eines objektbezogenen Vokabulars."

73 Idem, "Drei Schweizer Künstler. Roland Werro, Markus Raetz, Herbert Distel," in: *Art International*, 13, 1969, no. 1, Paris: Archive Press, pp. 39–43, here p. 40.

74 Stephan Kunz, "'Bossibulland'. Landschaft im Werk von Markus Raetz," in: *Markus Raetz. Zeichnungen*, catalog of the exhibition at the Kupferstichkabinett, Kunstmuseum Basel, October 20, 2012 to February 17, 2013, Ostfildern: Hatje Cantz, 2012, pp. 112–122, here p. 113.

75 Provence-Alpes-Côte d'Azur region, department of the Var.

76 Bernhard Bürgi, "Gesichtskreise," in: *Markus Raetz: Biennale di Venezia 1988, Svizzera*, catalog of the exhibition at the Swiss Pavilion, Venice Biennale, June 26 to September 25, 1988, Bern: Bundesamt für Kulturpflege, unpaginated: "magischen Schnitt durch alle Dimensionen, an dem sich die Reflexionen als Phänomene des Lichtes wie des Geistes brechen."

77 Müller 2023 (as note 2), no. 400. The material in this work is not sheet metal but buckskin mounted on a stretcher. The surface of the buckskin was "deformed" by brushing the nap in various directions with a finger, starting from the horizon line. This creates an extremely subtle relief.

78 Heinrich von Kleist, "Empfindungen vor Friedrichs Seelandschaft" (first published

[44] Toni Stooss, «Einleitung. Vom Leinwandknick zum *Zeemansblik*», in: *Markus Raetz. Arbeiten 1962 bis 1986* (Ausst.-Kat. Kunsthaus Zürich), Zürich: Edition Stähli, 1986, S. 7–9, Zitat S. 7.

[45] Gilbert Lascault, «Notizen zu einem Raetz-Dictionnaire», in: ebd., S. 53–61, Zitat S. 60.

[46] Müller 2023 (wie Anm. 2), Nr. 493.

[47] *Markus Raetz: Polaroïds 1978–1993*, Vorwort: Ad Petersen, Genf, Musée d'art et d'histoire, 1994 (erschienen anlässlich der Ausstellung *Markus Raetz* im IVAM, Centro Julio González, València [7.10.1993–2.1.1994], in der Serpentine Gallery, London [16.3.–24.4.1994] und im Musée Rath, Genf [17.6.–11.9.1994]), S. 85.

[48] Ebd., S. 94.

[49] So lautet der Untertitel seiner Einleitung zum Ausstellungskatalog der Raetz-Ausstellung von 1986 im Kunsthaus Zürich (wie Anm. 44).

[50] Müller 2023 (wie Anm. 2), Nr. 45, 48.

[51] Ein Relief trägt als Folge dieser Motivassoziation den Titel *La Cacahouète* (Müller 2023 [wie Anm. 2], Nr. 66).

[52] Ebd., Nr. 68.

[53] Jürgen Glaesemer, «Über die Zeichnungen von Markus Raetz», in: ders. *«Das Beobachten des Beobachtens». Markus Raetz. Zeichnungen*, Bern: Kunstmuseum, 1977, S. 9–30, hier S. 9.

[54] Raetz in einem Interview mit Hans-Joachim Müller, in: *Prix Meret Oppenheim 2006. Gamboni, Raetz, Schelbert, Suermondt, Winnewisser, Zumthor*, Bern: Bundesamt für Kultur, 2007, S. 25–37, Zitat S. 28.

[55] Raetz im Dokumentarfilm *Markus Raetz*, ein Film von Iwan Schumacher, Zürich: Schumacher & Frey, 2007, hier zit. nach Walter Keller, «Markus Raetz: falsch betrachtet – richtig gesehen», in: *Du*, 68, 2008/09, S. 104–111, Zitat S. 105. Zu *Eva*: Müller 2023 (wie Anm. 2), Nr. 226.

[56] Publiziert als Faksimile: Markus Raetz, *Die Bücher*, Zürich: Galerie und Edition Stähli, 1975, Band 2, o. S.

[57] Ebd., Band 3, o. S.

[58] Ernst Mach, *Die Analyse der Empfindungen und das Verhältnis des Physischen zum Psychischen*, 2. Aufl., Jena: Fischer, 1900, S. 15, Abb. 1.

[59] Die Illustration aus Machs Buch und Raetz' Zeichnung sind abgebildet in: Glaesemer 1977 (wie Anm. 53), S. 19.

[60] Mason 2023 (wie Anm. 8), Nr. 233, zweiter Zustand.

[61] Müller 2023 (wie Anm. 2), Nr. 677.

[62] Zeichnung vom 26.7.1985, reproduziert in: Gilbert Lascault, «Die Augen und das Sehen in einigen Werken von Markus Raetz» / «The Eyes, the Sight, in Some Works by Markus Raetz» / «Les Yeux, la vue, á partir de certaines œuvres de Markus Raetz», in: *Parkett*, 8, 1986, S. 30–36, Abb. S. 31.

[63] Lascault 1986a (wie Anm. 45), S. 53–61, Zitat S. 54.

[64] Lascault 1986b (wie Anm. 62), S. 30–36, Zitat S. 30.

[65] Die Zeichnung ist datiert mit 24./25.7. 1985, abgebildet in: Gilbert Lascault, «Fugues et variations des lignes», in: *Markus Raetz* (Ausst.-Kat. Carré d'Art – Musée d'art contemporain, Nîmes), Arles: Actes Sud, 2006, S. 9–43, Abb. S. 39.

[66] Zusätzlich zur Zeichnung vom 26.7.1985 ist in Lascault 1986b (wie Anm. 62), S. 30–36, Abb. S. 42, ein weiteres Blatt mit der Datierung 24.7.1985 mit dem Maskenmotiv reproduziert.

[67] Müller 2023 (wie Anm. 2), Nr. 344.

[68] Auch im Werk von Raetz findet sich die Parallelisierung oder Engführung von Kunst und Gewaltverbrechen. Auf einem kleinen dunkeltonigen Bild (Müller 2023 [wie Anm. 2], Nr. 484.22) sind zwei Rückenfiguren mit dem aufgemalten Buchstaben M und zwei liegende Figuren nebeneinander angeordnet. Die eine Figur hält einen Pinsel, die andere ein Messer in der erhobenen Hand. Der Buchstabe M auf dem Rücken des Malers und des Mörders steht gleichermassen für Malerei, Mord, Markus und Manet, denn die zwei liegenden männlichen Körper sind ein Zitat aus Edouard Manets Gemälde *L'homme mort* von 1864/65 (National Gallery of Art, Washington, DC). Der Buchstabe M ist zudem eine Referenz an den deutschen Filmklassiker von 1931 *M – Eine Stadt sucht einen Mörder* von Fritz Lang (1890–1976) oder an Alfred Hitchcocks (1899–1980) Thriller *Dial M for Murder* von 1954.

[69] Markus Ratz,«Wölflis Formenvokabular. Gezeichnet von Markus Rätz», in: *Adolf Wölfli. Schreiber, Dichter, Zeichner, Componist*, mit Texten von Daniel Baumann (et al.), hrsg. von der Adolf-Wölfli-Stiftung, Kunstmuseum Bern, Basel: Wiese Verlag, 1996, S. 226–227.

[70] Abgebildet in: Lascault 1986b (wie Anm. 62), Abb. S. 42.

[71] Lagger 2014 (wie Anm. 25), S. 10.

[72] Jean-Christophe Ammann, «Fünf junge Berner Künstler: Werro, Raetz, Fivian, Gertsch, Distel», in: *Das Werk*, 55, 1968, S. 245–250, Zitat S. 245.

[73] Jean-Christophe Ammann, «Drei Schweizer Künstler. Roland Werro, Markus Raetz, Herbert Distel», in: *Art International*, 13, 1, 1969, Paris: Archive Press, S. 39–43, Zitat S. 40.

[74] Stephan Kunz, «‹Bossibulland›. Landschaft im Werk von Markus Raetz», in: *Markus Raetz. Zeichnungen* (Ausst.-Kat. Kunstmuseum Basel, Kupferstichkabinett, 20.10.2012–17.2.2013), Ostfildern: Hatje Cantz, 2012, S. 112–122, Zitat S. 113.

[75] Region Provence-Alpes-Côte d'Azur, Departement Var.

[76] Bernhard Bürgi, «Gesichtskreise», in: *Markus Raetz: Biennale di Venezia 1988, Svizzera* (Ausst.-Kat. Venedig, 26.6.–25.9.1988), Bern: Bundesamt für Kulturpflege, o. S.

[77] Müller 2023 (wie Anm. 2), Nr. 400. Das Material ist bei diesem Werk nicht Blech, sondern über einen Spannrahmen fixiertes Wildleder, dessen raue Oberfläche mit dem Finger von der Horizontlinie ausgehend in verschiedene Richtungen «verformt» wurde und dadurch ein extrem feines Relief bildet.

[78] Heinrich von Kleist, «Empfindungen vor Friedrichs Seelandschaft» (erstmals veröffentlicht 1810), in: ders., *Das Erdbeben in Chili, Das Bettelweib von Locarno, Die heilige Cäcilie, Über das Marionettentheater, und andere Prosastücke*, Stuttgart: Reclam, 1979, S. 67–68, Zitat S. 68.

[79] Lagger 2014 (wie Anm. 25), S. 11.

[80] Jürgen Glaesemer, «Wie Erfindungen vom Fleck kommen», in: *Parkett*, 8, 1986, S. 66–75, hier S. 69.

[81] Zit. nach der Übersetzung von Werner Busch, in: ders., *Landschaftsmalerei*, Berlin: Reimer, 1997, S. 206–210, Zitat S. 208.

[82] Ebd., S. 209.

[83] Als einzige Beschichtung auf dem säureempfindlichen Blech empfahl Raetz einen dünnen Film aus säurefreiem Öl, z. B. Vaselineöl (Markus Raetz, Installationsanleitung für *Zeemansblik*, 27.8.1999).

[84] Jean-Luc Monterosso, «Ein photographisches Abc», in: *Markus Raetz. Nothing is Lighter than Light* (Ausst.-Kat. Aargauer Kunsthaus, Aarau, 4.6.–28.8.2005), Aarau: Aargauer Kunsthaus, o. S.

[85] Marcia Tucker, «Markus Raetz. In the Realm of the Possible», in: *Markus Raetz. In the Realm of the Possible* (Ausst.-Kat. The New Museum of Contemporary Art, New York, 13.5.–10.7.1988), New York: The New Museum of Contemporary Art, 1988, S. 10–57, Zitat S. 13–14: «And perhaps the most pervasive series of ‹landscape› paintings in his work are neither landscapes nor paintings, but pieces of cut and bent tin, each of which he calls by the Dutch word *Zeemansblik* [...].»

[86] Lagger 2014 (wie Anm. 25), S. 10.

[87] Oskar Bätschmann, «Landschaften in Unschärfe», in: Dietmar Elger (Hg.), *Gerhard Richter. Landschaften*, Ostfildern: Hatje Cantz, 2011, S. 57–69, hier S. 63.

[88] Dieser Aspekt der ironischen Brechung traditioneller Kunst und ihrer Rezeption war Raetz wichtig. Vgl. Lagger 2014 (wie Anm. 25), hier S. 10. Raetz wies in seiner Installationsanleitung für *Zeemansblik* darauf hin, dass das Relief nicht einem Fenster gegenüber aufgehängt werden sollte.

[89] *The Box of 1914*, Schwarz 1997 (wie Anm. 36), Nr. 285.

[90] *Junggesellenmaschinen*, Kunsthalle Bern, 5.7.–17.8.1975; weitere Stationen bis 1977 Venedig, Brüssel, Düsseldorf, Paris, Malmö, Amsterdam und Wien. Kuratiert wurde die Ausstellung von Harald Szeemann.

[91] Müller 2023 (wie Anm. 2), Nr. 511–523, 556, 557, 563, 564, 566.

1810), in: *Das Erdbeben in Chili, Das Bettelweib von Locarno, Die heilige Cäcilie, Über das Marionettentheater, und andere Prosastücke*, Stuttgart: Reclam, 1979, pp. 67–68, here p. 68: "[...] und da es [das Bild], in seiner Einförmigkeit und Uferlosigkeit, nichts, als den Rahm, zum Vordergrund hat, so ist es, wenn man es betrachtet, als ob einem die Augenlider weggeschnitten wären."

79 Lagger 2014 (as note 25), p. 11: "Spielraum zum Erfinden."

80 Jürgen Glaesemer, "Wie Erfindungen vom Fleck kommen" / "How invention derives from the blot," in: *Parkett*, 8, 1986, p. 66–75 (German), pp. 76–81 (English), here p. 78.

81 Alexander Cozens, A *New Method of Assisting the Invention in Drawing Original Compositions of Landscape*, London: J. Dixwell, undated [1785], p. 3.

82 Ibid., p. 13.

83 The only coating Raetz recommended for the acid-sensitive sheet metal was a thin film of acid-free oil, e.g., Vaseline oil (Markus Raetz, installation instructions for *Zeemansblik*, August 27, 1999).

84 Jean-Luc Monterosso, "Ein photographisches Abc," in: *Markus Raetz. Nothing is Lighter than Light*, catalog of the exhibition at the Aargauer Kunsthaus, Aarau, June 4 to August 28, 2005, unpaginated: "Ein Marinebild ohne Malerei."

85 Marcia Tucker, "Markus Raetz. In the Realm of the Possible," in: *Markus Raetz. In the Realm of the Possible*, catalog of the exhibition at the New Museum of Contemporary Art, New York, May 13 to July 10, 1988, New York: The New Museum of Contemporary Art, 1988, pp. 10–57, here pp. 13–14.

86 Lagger 2014 (as note 25), p. 10: "ein zu wenig intimes Verhältnis zur Farbe."

87 Oskar Bätschmann, "Landschaften in Unschärfe," in: Dietmar Elger (ed.), *Gerhard Richter. Landschaften*, Ostfildern: Hatje Cantz, 2011, pp. 57–69, here p. 63.

88 This aspect, with its ironic take on traditional art and its reception, was important to Raetz: cf. Lagger 2014 (as note 25), p. 10. In his installation instructions for *Zeemansblik*, Raetz stated that the relief should not be hung opposite a window.

89 *The Box of 1914*, Schwarz 1997 (as note 36), no. 285.

90 *Junggesellenmaschinen*, Kunsthalle Bern, July 5–August 17, 1975; over the next two years, the exhibition traveled to Venice, Brussels, Düsseldorf, Paris, Malmö, Amsterdam, and Vienna.

91 Müller 2023 (as note 2), nos. 511–523, 556, 557, 563, 564, 566.

92 Ibid., no. 1137; Schwarz 1997 (as note 36), no. 557. Duchamp used his collage as the basis for further works: ibid., nos. 565, 582.

93 Jürgen Glaesemer cited this phrase in the title of his 1977 publication *"'Das Beobachten des Beobachtens'." Markus Raetz. Zeichnungen* (as note 53).

94 A number of examples are illustrated in: Lascault 1986b (as note 62).

95 Raetz treats this motif not only in many drawings, but also in three prints. See Mason 2014 (as note 8), nos. 229–231.

96 Dario Gamboni, *Potential Images. Ambiguity and Indeterminacy in Modern Art*, London: Reaktion Books, 2002, p. 232, interprets Raetz's drawn variations on the motif of the ray of vision as representations of the "extramissive hypothesis."

97 Müller 2023 (as note 2), no. 550.

98 Ibid., nos. 1162, 1163, 1165, 1167. In these works, however, the shape of the cone can also be understood as a cylinder or round-ended cylinder represented in perspective.

99 Ibid., no. 1173, where one of the drawings is also reproduced. On the basis of the artist's sketched instructions, the filigree cone cloud was created for the first time at the first posthumous Raetz retrospective, *MARKUS RAETZ. oui non si no yes no*, September 8, 2023 to February 25, 2024, at the Kunstmuseum Bern. The photographer and artist Alexander Jaquemet, who had been photographing Raetz's works for more than ten years and is familiar with his art, was responsible for its installation. The exhibition was curated by Stephan Kunz, artistic director of the Bündner Kunstmuseum, Chur.

100 Ibid., no. 549.

101 Ibid., nos. 458, 459, 464, 484.3.

102 Ibid., no. 495.

103 Ibid., no. 484. The installation of twenty-four parts, including two upholstered benches, is untitled.

104 Dieter Koepplin, Room Guide accompanying the exhibition *Markus Raetz. Installation, Zeichnungen*, Museum für Gegenwartskunst, Basel, July 29 to September 25, 1989: "alles andere als abstraktes Thema: Sehen."

105 Ibid.: "Seh-Räume"; "Wege des Sehens [...] in Räumen, die zugleich innen und aussen waren, zugleich Höhlen und weiteste Horizonte gaben."

106 Ibid.: "jenen schlichten, beruhigenden oder auch immer wieder aufwühlenden, dramatischen Meereshorizont [...], der die meditativen Romantiker ebenso in Bann zog wie die tatkräftigen Abenteurer."

107 Müller 2023 (as note 2), nos. 572–573, 575–580, 584, 586–593. One sculpture is made of slate (no. 585). No. 594 was created in 1989, and no. 597 is a 1994 steel cast from a wax model. No. 579 served as the basis for an edition in cast iron titled *Fernseh* (no. 583), and no. 580 for two editions in cast brass and cast iron respectively, both titled *Fernsicht* (nos. 581–582). As variants of the motif, no. 574 shows a man holding a photo camera or film camera in front of his eyes, and nos. 595 and 596 show a man shading his eyes with his hand to sharpen his gaze. These two last sculptures bear the respective titles *Das bessere Sehen* (Better Seeing) and *Besser sehen* (Seeing Better).

108 Kleist 1979 (as note 78), p. 68: "Herrlich ist es in einer unendlichen Einsamkeit am Meeresufer, unter trübem Himmel, auf eine unbegrenzte Wasserwüste, hinauszuschauen. [...] und so ward ich selbst der Kapuziner, das Bild ward die Düne, das aber, wo hinaus ich mit Sehnsucht blicken sollte, die See, fehlte ganz."

109 Ibid.: "Nichts kann trauriger und unbehaglicher sein, als diese Stellung in der Welt: der einzige Lebensfunke im weiten Reich des Todes, der einsame Mittelpunkt im einsamen Kreis."

110 Müller 2023 (as note 2), no. 582.5.

111 Ibid., no. 581.

112 Ibid., no. 580.

113 "Feldstechermann" manuscript, Estate of Markus Raetz, Bern. Adolf Wölfli, *Von der Wiege bis zum Graab. Oder, Durch arbeiten und schwitzen, leiden, und Drangsal bettend zum Fluch. Schriften 1908–1912*, vol. 1, published by the Adolf-Wölfli-Stiftung, Kunstmuseum Bern, Frankfurt am Main: Fischer, 1985, p. 19, no. 2, p. 456, no. 76b. Among Raetz's drawings based on Wölfli's formal vocabulary are motifs of spectacles and faces with mask-like outlines around the eyes, which approximate the shape of the *Zeemansblik* binocular field of view (see illustrations in Raetz 1996 [as note 69], p. 227).

114 *Die Schwerkraft der Berge*, ed. Stephan Kunz, Beat Wismer, and Wolfgang Denk, catalog of the exhibition at the Aargauer Kunsthaus, Aarau, June 15 to August 24, 1997, and the Kunsthalle Krems, September 7 to November 23, 1997, Basel/Frankfurt am Main: Stroemfeld/Roter Stern, 1997. The four *Fernsicht* sculptures on display were Müller 2023 (as note 2), nos. 585, 586, 594 and one copy of no. 582.

115 In the major 2023/24 exhibition at the Kunstmuseum Bern (as note 99), however, the Aarau *Zeemansblik* was paired with a different pendant, namely Müller 2023 (as note 2), no. 583.2.

116 Müller 2023 (as note 2), no. 1037.

117 *Ich sehe ein Bild*, 1977, glue mixed with pigment on cotton (sheet), ca. 250 × 169 cm, Estate of Markus Raetz, Bern.

118 Raetz 2007 (as note 54), p. 29: "eigentliches Thema," "ein Reservoir an zweidimensionalen Formen."

119 Ibid.: "zweidimensionale Netzhautbild."

120 Max Wechsler, "Das Bild vom Bild im Bild des Bildes," in: *Künstler. Kritisches Lexikon der*

[92] Ebd., Nr. 1137; Schwarz 1997 (wie Anm. 36), Nr. 557. Duchamp benutzte die Collage bis 1962 als Grundlage weiterer Werke: ebd., Nr. 565, 582.

[93] Jürgen Glaesemer übernahm diesen Begriff von Raetz als Titel der Publikation über Raetz' Zeichnungen, die 1977 zu seiner Ausstellung im Kunstmuseum Bern erschien: *«Das Beobachten des Beobachtens». Markus Raetz. Zeichnungen* (wie Anm. 53).

[94] Einige Beispiele sind abgebildet in: Lascault 1986b (wie Anm. 62).

[95] Neben vielen Zeichnungen gibt es auch drei Druckgrafiken mit diesem Motiv. Mason 2014 (wie Anm. 8), Nr. 229–231.

[96] Dario Gamboni, *Potential Images. Ambiguity and Indeterminacy in Modern Art*, London: Reaktion Books, 2002, S. 232, interpretiert Raetz' gezeichnete Variationen auf das Motiv des Sehstrahls als Darstellungen der «extramissive hypothesis».

[97] Müller 2023 (wie Anm. 2), Nr. 550.

[98] Ebd., Nr. 1162, 1163, 1165, 1167. Die Form des Konus ist bei diesen Werken aber auch als perspektivisch dargestellter Zylinder oder Kugelzylinder zu verstehen.

[99] Ebd., Nr. 1173. Dort ist auch eine der Zeichnungen abgebildet. Für die erste postume Retrospektive *MARKUS RAETZ. oui non si no yes no*, 8.9.2023–25.2.2024 im Kunstmuseum Bern, wurde die filigrane Konus-Wolke auf der Grundlage der skizzierten Installationsanleitungen zum ersten Mal umgesetzt. Für die Realisierung war der Fotograf und Künstler Alexander Jaquemet verantwortlich, der mehr als zehn Jahre für Raetz Werkaufnahmen machte und mit seinen Arbeiten vertraut ist. Kurator der Ausstellung war Stephan Kunz, künstlerischer Direktor des Bündner Kunstmuseums, Chur.

[100] Ebd., Nr. 549.

[101] Ebd., Nr. 458, 459, 464, 484.3.

[102] Ebd., Nr. 495.

[103] Ebd., Nr. 484. Die Installation aus 24 Teilen, zu denen auch zwei gepolsterte Sitzbänke gehören, hat keinen Titel.

[104] Dieter Koepplin, Saalblatt zur Ausstellung *Markus Raetz. Installation, Zeichnungen*, Museum für Gegenwartskunst, Basel, 29.7.–25.9.1989.

[105] Ebd.

[106] Ebd.

[107] Müller 2023 (wie Anm. 2), Nr. 572–573, 575–580, 584, 586–593. Eine Skulptur besteht aus Schiefer (Nr. 585). Nr. 594 entstand 1989, Nr. 597 ist ein Stahlguss von 1994 nach einem Wachsmodell. Von den Fassungen Nr. 580 und 579 entstanden Auflagen in Messing- und Eisenguss unter den Titeln *Fernsicht* und *Fernseh* (Nr. 581–583). Als Motivvarianten zeigen Nr. 574 einen Mann, der sich einen Fotoapparat oder eine Filmkamera vor die Augen hält, und Nr. 595 und 596 einen Mann, der sich zur Schärfung des Blicks die Augen mit der Hand beschattet. Die beiden Skulpturen tragen die bezeichnenden Titel *Das bessere Sehen* und *Besser sehen*.

[108] Kleist 1979 (wie Anm. 78), S. 68.

[109] Ebd.

[110] Müller 2023 (wie Anm. 2), Nr. 582.5.

[111] Ebd., Nr. 581.

[112] Ebd., Nr. 580.

[113] Manuskript «Feldstechermann», Nachlass Markus Raetz, Bern. Adolf Wölfli, *Von der Wiege bis zum Graab. Oder, Durch arbeiten und schwitzen, leiden, und Drangsal bettend zum Fluch. Schriften 1908–1912*, Bd. 1, hg. von der Adolf-Wölfli-Stiftung, Kunstmuseum Bern, Frankfurt a. M.: Fischer, 1985, S. 19, Nr. 2, S. 456, Nr. 76b. Unter Raetz' Zeichnungen nach Wölflis Formenvokabular befinden sich Brillenmotive und Gesichter mit maskenartiger Umrandung der Augenpartie, die der Form des binokularen Gesichtsfeldes von *Zeemansblik* nahekommt (Abb. in: Raetz 1996 [wie Anm. 69], S. 227).

[114] *Die Schwerkraft der Berge* (Ausst.-Kat. Aargauer Kunsthaus, Aarau, 15.6.–24.8.1997 und Kunsthalle Krems, 7.9.–23.11.1997), hg. von Stephan Kunz, Beat Wismer und Wolfgang Denk, Basel etc.: Stroemfeld/Roter Stern, 1997. Ausgestellt waren Müller 2023 (wie Anm. 2), Nr. 585, 586, 594 und ein Ex. von Nr. 582.

[115] In der grossen Ausstellung im Kunstmuseum Bern (wie Anm. 99) wurde jedoch für den Aarauer *Zeemansblik* mit der Fassung Müller 2023 (wie Anm. 2), Nr. 583.2, ein anderes Pendant gewählt.

[116] Müller 2023 (wie Anm. 2), Nr. 1037.

[117] *Ich sehe ein Bild*, 1977, Leim mit Pigment vermischt auf Baumwolle (Leintuch), ca. 250 × 169 cm, Nachlass Markus Raetz, Bern.

[118] Raetz 2007 (wie Anm. 54), S. 29.

[119] Ebd.

[120] Max Wechsler, «Das Bild vom Bild im Bild des Bildes», in: *Künstler. Kritisches Lexikon der Gegenwartskunst*, München: Weltkunst/Bruckmann, 1989, S. 3.

[121] Bernd Hüppauf und Christoph Wulf, «Einleitung. Warum Bilder die Einbildungskraft brauchen», in: dies. (Hg.), *Bild und Einbildungskraft*, München: Wilhelm Fink, 2006, S. 9–44, Zitate S. 24.

[122] E. H. Gombrich, *Kunst und Illusion. Zur Psychologie der bildlichen Darstellung*, Köln: Phaidon, 1967[2], S. 271.

[123] Ebd., S. 228.

[124] Ebd., S. 271, 297.

[125] Walter Benjamin, «Das Kunstwerk im Zeitalter seiner technischen Reproduzierbarkeit», in: ders., *Das Kunstwerk im Zeitalter seiner technischen Reproduzierbarkeit. Drei Studien zur Kunstsoziologie*, Frankfurt a. M.: Suhrkamp, 1977, S. 7–44, hier S. 15. Eine solche ironische Bezugnahme von Raetz ist nicht ganz von der Hand zu weisen. Für seine Mickey-Mouse-Anamorphose *Diesseitig bin ich gar nicht fassbar* von 1974 beispielsweise profanierte er einen Teil der pathetischen Grabinschrift von Paul Klee (Müller 2023 [wie Anm. 2], Nr. 165).

[126] Gombrich 1967 (wie Anm. 119), S. 270.

[127] Müller 2023 (wie Anm. 122), Nr. 588.

[128] Gottfried Boehm, «Unbestimmtheit. Zur Logik des Bildes», in: Hüppauf/Wulf 2006 (wie Anm. 121), S. 243–253, hier S. 244.

[129] Ebd., S. 252. Hervorhebungen im Original.

[130] Ebd., S. 244; Gombrich 1967 (wie Anm. 122), S. 203.

[131] Bernhard Bürgi, *Markus Raetz. Die Bücher 1972–1976*, Zürich: Edition Stähli, 1987, Bd. 1, S. 30.

[132] Boehm 2006 (wie Anm. 128), S. 244.

[133] Bürgi 1987 (wie Anm. 131), Band I, S. 24–25.

[134] Jurgis Baltrušaitis, *Imaginäre Realitäten. Fiktion und Illusion als produktive Kraft*, Köln: DuMont, 1984, zum Phänomen der «Bilder im Stein»: S. 55–89.

[135] Glaesemer 1986 (wie Anm. 80), S. 73.

[136] Gamboni 2002 (wie Anm. 96).

[137] Horst Bredekamp, *Theorie des Bildakts*, Frankfurter Adorno-Vorlesungen 2007, Berlin: Suhrkamp, 2010, S. 320.

[138] Ebd., S. 9.

[139] Dieter Koepplin (Koepplin 1989b, wie Anm. 104) bezeichnete die *Zeemansblik*-Reliefs auch als «Wetterbleche (den akustischen Theaterdonnerblechen vielleicht ein wenig verwandt, aber völlig untheatralisch).»

[140] Gamboni 2002 (wie Anm. 96), S. 232.

Gegenwartskunst, Munich: Weltkunst/Bruckmann, 1989, p. 3: "Welt-Wirklichkeit," "Bild-Wirklichkeit."

121 Bernd Hüppauf and Christoph Wulf, "Einleitung. Warum Bilder die Einbildungskraft brauchen," in: idem (eds.), *Bild und Einbildungskraft*, Munich: Wilhelm Fink 2006, pp. 9–44, here p. 24: "Wahrnehmen lässt sich vom Imaginieren nicht trennen"; "Die Imagination versetzt ins Bild, was in der Datenvielfalt der Sinnenreize abwesend ist und ergänzt das stets nur partiell gegebene Bild zu einem Ganzen – ohne eine kreative Einbildungskraft kein sinnvolles und zusammenhängendes Bild."

122 E. H. Gombrich, *Art and Illusion. A Study in the Psychology of Pictorial Representation*, Oxford: Phaidon, 1977[5], p. 204.

123 Ibid., p. 170.

124 Ibid., pp. 205, 225.

125 Walter Benjamin, "The Work of Art in the Age of Mechanical Reproduction" (1935), in: Hannah Arendt (ed.), *Illuminations*, trans. Harry Zohn, New York: Schocken Books, 1969, pp. 1–26, here p. 5. The possibility that Raetz was making an ironic reference of this kind cannot be entirely dismissed. For his 1974 Mickey Mouse anamorphosis *Diesseitig bin ich gar nicht fassbar* (I cannot be grasped in the here and now), for example, he secularized the first line of the pathos-laden epitaph on Paul Klee's tombstone (Müller 2023 [as note 2], no. 165).

126 Gombrich 1977 (as note 122), p. 204.

127 Müller 2023 (as note 2), no. 588. The original inscription in German reads "WAS ER SIEHT."

128 Gottfried Boehm, "Unbestimmtheit. Zur Logik des Bildes," in: Hüppauf/Wulf 2006 (as note 121), pp. 243–253, here p. 244.

129 Ibid., p. 252, emphasis in the original.

130 Ibid., p. 244; Gombrich 1977, p. 203.

131 Bernhard Bürgi, *Markus Raetz. Die Bücher 1972–1976*, Zurich: Edition Stähli, 1987, vol. 1, p. 30.

132 Boehm 2006 (as note 128), p. 244.

133 Bürgi 1987 (as note 131), vol. 1, pp. 24f.

134 Jurgis Baltrušaitis, *Imaginäre Realitäten. Fiktion und Illusion als produktive Kraft*, Cologne: DuMont, 1984. On the phenomenon of pictures in stone: pp. 55–89.

135 Glaesemer 1986 (as note 80), p. 80.

136 Gamboni 2002 (as note 96).

137 Horst Bredekamp, *Theorie des Bildakts*, Frankfurt Adorno-Vorlesungen 2007, Berlin: Suhrkamp 2010, p. 320: "in die Moderne und deren Faible für die Eigenmotorik der abstrakten Form."

138 Ibid., p. 9: "den Zufallsbildern der Wolkengebirge."

139 Dieter Koepplin (Koepplin 1989b, as note 104) also described the *Zeemansblik* reliefs as "weather sheets (perhaps a little related to the thunder sheets used for theatrical sound effects, but completely untheatrical)."

140 Gamboni 2002 (as note 96), p. 232.

Ausgewählte Bibliografie / Selected Bibliography

Jean-Christophe Ammann, «Drei Schweizer Künstler: Roland Werro, Markus Raetz, Herbert Distel», in: *Art International*, Bd. / vol. 13, Nr. / no. 1, 1969, S. / pp. 39–43.

Markus Raetz. Zeichnungen, Objekte, mit Beitr. von / with contributions by Dieter Koepplin (Ausst.-Kat. / exhib. cat., Kunstmuseum Basel, 4.3.–16.4.1972), Basel: Kunstmuseum Basel, 1972.

Theo Kneubühler, *Kunst: 28 Schweizer*, Luzern: Edition Galerie Raeber, 1972.

Markus Raetz, *Notizbüchlein 27. Aug. 1971 bis 17. Sept. 1971*, Amsterdam, hrsg. von / ed. by Toni Gerber und / and P. B. Stähli, Luzern, 1972.

Markus Raetz. Zeichnungen, Aquarelle, «Die Bücher», mit Beitr. von / with contributions by Wilfried Skreiner und / and Jean-Christophe Ammann (Ausst.-Kat. / exhib. cat., Neue Galerie am Landesmuseum Joanneum, Graz, 24.10.–30.11.1975), Graz: Akademische Druck- und Verlagsanstalt, 1975.

Markus Raetz, *Markus Raetz. Die Bücher*, 3 Bde. / vols., Zürich: Galerie & Edition Stähli, 1975.

Notizbuch. Amsterdam Frühjahr 1973. Arbeiten aus einem Monat und einer Nacht von Markus Raetz, mit Beitr. von / with contributions by Erika Gysling-Billeter (Ausst.-Kat. / exhib. cat., Kunsthaus Zürich, 4.10.–2.11.1975), Zürich: Kunsthaus Zürich, 1975.

Toni Gerber, *Bezüge und Beziehungen. Ein Text zu Arbeiten von Markus Raetz*, Reinach: Edition Schaub, 1977.

& u. & + &, mit Beitr. von / with contributions by Rolf Geissbühler, Bern: Kunsthalle Bern, 1977.

«Das Beobachten des Beobachtens». Markus Raetz. Zeichnungen, mit Beitr. von / with contributions by Jürgen Glaesemer, Bern: Kunstmuseum Bern, 1977.

Markus Raetz, 2 Bde. / vols. [deutsch, niederländisch] (Ausst.-Kat. / exhib. cat., Stedelijk Museum, Amsterdam, 6.4.–20.5.1979), Amsterdam: Stedelijk Museum, 1979.

[Markus Raetz], *Mimi*, Zürich: Galerie & Edition Stähli, 1981.

Markus Raetz. Arbeiten. Travaux. Works 1971–1981, mit Beitr. von / with contributions by Jean-Christophe Ammann (Ausst.-Kat. / exhib. cat., Kunsthalle Basel, 2.10.–7.11.1982; Musée d'art moderne de la Ville de Paris, 27.1.–6.3.1983; Nouveau Musée, Villeurbanne, 18.3.–15.5.1983; Frankfurter Kunstverein, Frankfurt a. M., 24.6.–24.7.1983), Basel: Kunsthalle Basel, 1982.

Markus Raetz, *Notizen 1981–82*, Zürich: Galerie & Edition Stähli / Berlin: Rainer Verlag / Künstlerprogramm DAAD, 1982.

Jürgen Glaesemer, «Wie Erfindungen vom Fleck kommen / How Invention Derives from the Blot», in: *Parkett*, Nr. / no. 8, 1986, S. 66–81 / pp. 76–80.

Gilbert Lascault, «Die Augen und das Sehen in einigen Werken von Markus Raetz / The Eyes, the Sight, in Some Works by Markus Raetz», in: *Parkett*, Nr. / no. 8, 1986, S. 30–45 / pp. 38–42 [frz. Übers. S. 43–45].

Markus Raetz. Arbeiten 1962 bis 1986, hrsg. von / ed. by Bernhard Bürgi und / and Toni Stooss (Ausst.-Kat. / exhib. cat., Kunsthaus Zürich, 13.6.–17.8.1986; Kölnischer Kunstverein, Köln, 7.12.1986–4.1.1987; Moderna Museet, Stockholm, 25.4.–7.6.1987), Zürich: Edition Stähli, 1986.

Bern 66 → 1987 (Ausst.-Kat. / exhib. cat., Kunsthalle Bern, 28.3.–17.5.1987), Bern: Kunsthalle Bern, 1987.

Bernhard Bürgi, *Markus Raetz. Die Bücher 1972–1976*, 2 Bde. / vols., Zürich: Edition Stähli, 1987.

Walter Grasskamp, «Markus Raetz. Der Pförtner der Wahrnehmung», in: *Kunst-Bulletin*, Nr. / no. 11, 1987, S. / pp. 6–11.

Markus Raetz: In the Realm of the Possible, mit Beitr. von / with contributions by Marcia Tucker (Ausst.-Kat. / exhib. cat., New Museum of Contemporary Art, New York, 13.5.–10.7.1988), New York: Museum of Contemporary Art, 1988.

Markus Raetz, mit Beitr. von / with contributions by Bernhard Bürgi, (Ausst.-Kat. / exhib. cat., Schweizer Pavillon, Venedig, 26.6.–25.9.1988), Bern: Bundesamt für Kulturpflege, 1988.

Hans Christoph von Tavel, «Markus Raetz. Ohne Titel, Rauminstallation, 1983», in: *Berner Kunstmitteilungen*, Nr. / no. 270, 1989, S. / pp. 13.

Max Wechsler, «Das Bild vom Bild im Bild des Bildes», in: *Künstler. Kritisches Lexikon der Gegenwartskunst*, Ausgabe 8 / Edition 8, München: Weltkunst/Bruckmann, 1989.

Christoph Doswald, «Interview mit Markus Raetz», in: *Kunstforum International*, Bd. / vol. 105, 1990, S./pp. 200–205.

Rainer Michael Mason und / and Juliane Willi-Cosandier, *Markus Raetz. Les estampes. Die Druckgrafik. The Prints, 1957–1991*, (Ausst.-Kat. / exhib. cat., Kunstmuseum Bern, 29.10.1991–5.1.1992; Cabinet des estampes, Musée d'art et d'histoire, Genf, 20.1.–22.3.1992), Zürich: Galerie & Edition Stähli, 1991.

Andreas Meier, «Das verlorene Profil – Markus Raetz' Hommage an Robert Walser», in: *Der Rabe*, Nr. / no. 32, 1992, S. / pp. 36–41.

Markus Raetz, mit Beitr. von / with contributions by Cäsar Menz et al., (Ausst.-Kat. / exhib. cat., IVAM Centre Julio Gonzalez, Valencia, 7.10.1993–2.1.1994; Serpentine Gallery, London, 16.3.–24.4.1994; Musée Rath, Genf, 17.6.–11.9.1994), Genf: Musées d'art et d'histoire, 1994.

Markus Raetz, (Ausst.-Kat. / exhib. cat., Museum of Contemporary Art KIASMA / Finnish National Gallery, Helsinki, 30.9.–13.11.1994), Helsinki: Museum of Contemporary Art, 1994.

Markus Raetz. Polaroids 1978–1993, mit Vorw. Von / with forew. by Ad Petersen, Genf: Musée d'art et d'histoire, 1994.

Max Wechsler, «Markus Raetz. Vom Fluss der Figurationen zwischen den Figuren», in: *Kunst-Bulletin*, Nr. / no. 4, 1994, S. / pp. 12–19.

Markus Raetz, hrsg. von / ed. by Andreas Meier und / and Centre PasquArt, (Ausst.-Kat. / exhib. cat., Centre PasquArt, Biel, 23.6.–2.9.2001), Bern: Stämpfli, 2001.

Markus Raetz, (Ausst.-Kat. / exhib. cat., The Arts Club of Chicago, 25.1.–7.4.2001; University Gallery, University of Massachusetts, Amherst, 15.9.–15.12. 2001), Chicago: The Arts Club of Chicago, 2001.

Place du Rhône, red. Von / ed. by Valérie Muller, mit Beitr. von / with contributions by Claude Ritschard, Genf: Ville de Genève, 2001.

Nothing Is Lighter than Light. Markus Raetz, mit Beitr. von / with contributions by Hervé Gauville, Jean-Luc Monterosso und / and Toni Stooss, (Ausst.-Kat. / exhib. cat., Maison Européenne de la Photographie, Paris, 12.12.2002–23.2.2003), Paris: Maison Européenne de la Photographie, 2002.

Markus Raetz. No W Here, mit Beitr. von / with contributions by Ursula Bode et al., (Ausst.-Kat. / exhib. cat., Lindenau-Museum Altenburg, 21.11.2004–20.2.2005), Nürnberg: Verlag für moderne Kunst, 2005.

Blickwechsel. Texte zum Werk von Markus Raetz, hrsg. von / ed. by Stephan Kunz, Aarau: Aargauer Kunsthaus / Nürnberg: Verlag für moderne Kunst, 2005.

Markus Raetz. Eben: 1971 / 2005, hrsg. von / ed. by Gianni Paravicini-Tönz und / and Flurina Paravicini-Tönz, mit Beitr. von / with contributions by Max Wechsler, Luzern: Periferia, 2005 [mit DVD von / with DVD by Markus Raetz].

Markus Raetz, mit Beitr. von / with contributions by Gilbert Lascault, (Ausst.-Kat. / exhib. cat., Musée d'art contemporain, Nîmes, 1.2.–7.5. 2006), Arles: Actes Sud, 2006.

Markus Raetz. Nothing Is Lighter than Light, hrsg. von / ed. by Toni Stooss, mit Beitr. von / with contributions by Hervé Gauville et al., (Ausst.-Kat. / exhib. cat., Museum der Moderne, Salzburg, 28.10.2006–4.2.2007), Salzburg: Museum der Moderne, 2006.

Hans-Joachim Müller, «Markus Raetz [Interview]», in: *Prix Meret Oppenheim 2006. Gamboni, Raetz, Schelbert, Suermondt, Winnewisser, Zumthor*, Bern: Bundesamt für Kultur, 2007, S. / pp. 25–37.

Bilderwahl! Metamorphose ... heute. Im Dialog mit Com&Com, Michael Günzburger, Lutz & Guggisberg, David Renggli und Tobias Spichtig, mit Beitr. von / with contributions by Jeannette E. Weiss, (Ausst.-Kat. / exhib. cat., Kunsthaus Zürich, 26.11.2010–27.2.2011), Zürich: Zürcher Kunstgesellschaft, 2010.

Markus Raetz. Estampes, sculptures. Prints, Sculptures, hrsg. von / ed. by Pierrette Crouzet, (Ausst.-Kat. / exhib. cat., Bibliothèque Nationale de France, Paris, 8.11.2011–12.2.2012; MUba Eugène Leroy, Tourcoing, 23.3.–11.6.2012), Paris: Bibliothèque nationale de France, 2011.

Markus Raetz. Zeichnungen, mit Beitr. von / with contributions by Anita Haldemann et al., (Ausst.-Kat. / exhib. cat., Kunstmuseum Basel, 20.10.2012–17.2.2013), Ostfildern: Hatje Cantz, 2012.

Markus Raetz. Die Druckgraphik. Les estampes. The prints. Catalogue raisonné 1951–2013, 2 Bde. / vols., hrsg. von / ed. by Rainer Michael Mason, in Zusammenarbeit mit / in collaboration with Claudine Metzger, Zürich: Scheidegger & Spiess, 2014.

Miriam Sturzenegger, «Miriam Sturzenegger im Gespräch mit Markus Raetz», in: Dora Imhof und / and Sibylle Omlin, *Kristallisationsorte der Kunst in der Schweiz. Aarau, Genf, Luzern in den 1970er-Jahren*, Zürich: Scheidegger & Spiess, 2014, S. / pp. 327–338.

Markus Raetz. Chambre de lecture, mit Beitr. von / with contributions by Marco Franciolli und / and Francesca Bernasconi, (Ausst.-Kat. / exhib. cat., Museo d'arte della Svizzera italiana, Lugano, 30.1.–1.5.2016, Lugano: MASI / Bellinzona: Edizioni Casagrande, 2016.

Rainer Michael Mason, *Markus Raetz. Le Palindrome. Dessins de l'artiste & repères de Rainer Michael Mason*, Bern: Till Schaap Edition, 2016.

Markus Raetz und / and Max Wechsler, *Impressions d'Impressions d'Afrique*, Luzern / Poschiavo: Edizioni Periferia, 2016.

Nina Zimmer, «Der Raetzsche Mimi-Malismus», in: *Freundeswerke. 100 Jahre Verein der Freunde Kunstmuseum Bern 1920–2020*, hrsg. von / ed. by Marie Therese Bätschmann, VdF, Bern: Till Schaap Edition, 2019, S. / pp. 199–203.

Markus Raetz. Le reflet des mots, mit Beitr. von / with contributions by Rainer Michael Mason (Ausst.-Kat. / exhib. cat., Fondation Jan Michalski, Montricher, 18.3.–10.7.2022), Montricher: Fondation Jan Michalski, 2022.

Markus Raetz. Atelier, hrsg. von / ed. by Stephan Kunz und / and Nina Zimmer, mit Beitr. von / with contributions by Stephan Kunz und / and Didier Semin, Fotografien von / photographs Alexander Jaquemet, Bern: Kunstmuseum / Zürich: Scheidegger & Spiess, 2023.

Franz Müller, *Markus Raetz. Das plastische Werk. Catalogue raisonné*, mit Beitr. von / with contributions by Katharina Ammann, Andrea Arnold und / and Patricia Bieder, 2 Bde. / vols., Zürich: Schweizerisches Institut für Kunstwissenschaft (SIK-ISEA) / Scheidegger & Spiess, 2023 (Œuvrekataloge Schweizer Künstler und Künstlerinnen 30).

Chronology

1941
Markus Raetz is born on June 6 in Bern and grows up with two older siblings in Büren an der Aare.

1957–1961
Trains as an elementary school teacher at the Hofwil teacher-training college in Münchenbuchsee. During vacations, he works in the studio of artist Peter Travaglini (1927–2015) in Büren. Internship in Oberbipp at a school for children and young people with behavioral problems. Caricatures for satirical magazines. In 1960, first exhibition at the Théâtre de Poche, Biel, with college colleague Bendicht Fivian (1940–2019).

1961–1963
Elementary school teacher in Brügg, near Biel. Creates his first relief pictures.

1963
Swiss Federal art scholarship. Gives up teaching. Moves to Bern.

1965
Swiss Federal art scholarship. Participates in the 4th Biennale des Jeunes in Paris with *Zone blanche*.

1966
Visits various artist studios in London with Harald Szeemann, director of the Kunsthalle Bern, and fellow Bern-based artists. Participates in the group exhibition *Bern 66* in Gelsenkirchen, with further stops in Bern and Rotterdam.

1967
First extended stay in Ramatuelle (South of France). Teaches the "F + F" ("Form + Farbe") art class at the Kunstgewerbeschule Zürich. Participates in the *Science Fiction* exhibition at the Kunsthalle Bern, with further stops in Paris and Düsseldorf. Awarded the City of Geneva's Prix de la jeune gravure suisse.

1968
Participates in the group exhibition *Wege und Experimente. 30 junge Schweizer Künstler* at the Kunsthaus Zürich and in documenta 4 in Kassel.

1969
Starts working with the photographer Balthasar Burkhard (1944–2010). Produces large-format photo canvases. Participates in the exhibitions *Live in Your Head: When Attitudes Become Form* at the Kunsthalle Bern and *22 jonge Zwitsers* at the Stedelijk Museum in Amsterdam. Beginning of friendship with the curator Ad Petersen (1931–2021). In June, moves to Amsterdam with his partner Monika Müller.

1970
Marriage to Monika Müller. Studies various etching techniques at the Rietveld Academie in Amsterdam. Participates in the exhibition *Visualisierte Denkprozesse* at the Kunstmuseum Luzern, and in exhibitions in New York and Tokyo.

1971
Spends several months in Andalusia and Morocco. Drawings for the animated film *eben*.

1972
Birth of daughter Aimée. First solo museum exhibition at the Kunstmuseum Basel, which subsequently travels to the Cabinet des estampes at the Musée d'art et d'histoire, Geneva. Participates in documenta 5 in Kassel.

1973
Exhibition at the Goethe Institute in Amsterdam. In summer, moves to Carona in Ticino. Meets Meret Oppenheim (1913–1985).

1974
Anamorphic room installation with the motif of the head of Mickey Mouse for the exhibition *Planetarium* at the Galerie Toni Gerber, Bern.

1975
Visits Egypt and Tunisia. Participates in Harald Szeemann's exhibition *Junggesellenmaschinen* at the Kunsthalle Bern, with further stops in Italy, Belgium, Germany, France, Sweden, Holland, and Austria. Solo exhibition at the Kunsthaus Zürich.

1976
Moves from Carona back to Bern.

1977
His Neugasse studio is destroyed by fire, with the loss of many works. Solo shows at the Kunsthalle Bern and the Kunstmuseum Bern. Produces the artist's book *& u. & + &* with his friends Walo von Fellenberg and Rolf Geissbühler. Jürgen Glaesemer publishes the first major monograph on Raetz's drawings. Participates in the Bienal de São Paulo. Starts working with the copper printer Peter Kneubühler (1944–1999) in Zurich.

1978
Moves into a new studio at 3, Sandrainstrasse, in Bern. From now until 2010, annual spring and fall visits to Ramatuelle.

1979
Studio in Amsterdam as a guest of the Stedelijk Museum, where he is given a solo exhibition.

1981
Solo exhibition at the Aargauer Kunsthaus, Aarau, which subsequently travels to Innsbruck and Vienna. Extended stay in Berlin as a guest of the DAAD German Academic Exchange Service (until 1982).

1982
Solo exhibitions in the DAAD-Galerie, Berlin, and in the Kunsthalle Basel. Participates in documenta 7 in Kassel. Installation of a large *MIMI* sculpture made of granite blocks in the Parc de la Cerisaie, Lyon.

Chronologie

1941
Markus Raetz wird am 6. Juni in Bern geboren und wächst mit zwei älteren Geschwistern in Büren an der Aare auf.

1957–1961
Ausbildung zum Primarlehrer am Lehrerseminar Hofwil, Münchenbuchsee. Jeweils in den Ferien Arbeit im Atelier des Künstlers Peter Travaglini (1927–2015) in Büren. Praktikum in Oberbipp in einer Schule für verhaltensauffällige Kinder und Jugendliche. Karikaturen für satirische Zeitschriften. 1960 erste Ausstellung im Théâtre de Poche, Biel, mit seinem Seminarkollegen Bendicht Fivian (1940–2019).

1961–1963
Primarlehrer in Brügg bei Biel. Es entstehen die ersten Reliefbilder.

1963
Eidgenössisches Kunststipendium. Gibt die Lehrtätigkeit auf. Umzug nach Bern.

1965
Eidgenössisches Kunststipendium. Teilnahme an der 4. Biennale des Jeunes in Paris mit *Zone blanche*.

1966
Mit Harald Szeemann, Leiter der Kunsthalle Bern, und Berner Künstlerkollegen Besuch verschiedener Künstlerateliers in London. Teilnahme an der Gruppenausstellung *Bern 66* in Gelsenkirchen, mit weiteren Stationen in Bern und Rotterdam.

1967
Erster längerer Aufenthalt in Ramatuelle (Südfrankreich). Unterrichtet an der Kunstgewerbeschule Zürich die Klasse F + F (Kunstklasse Form + Farbe). Teilnahme an der Ausstellung *Science Fiction* in der Kunsthalle Bern, weitere Stationen in Paris und Düsseldorf. Prix de la Jeune gravure suisse der Stadt Genf.

1968
Teilnahme an der Gruppenausstellung *Wege und Experimente. 30 junge Schweizer Künstler* im Kunsthaus Zürich und an der documenta 4 in Kassel.

1969
Beginn der Zusammenarbeit mit dem Fotografen Balthasar Burkhard (1944–2010). Es entstehen grossformatige Fotoleinwände. Teilnahme an den Ausstellungen *Live in Your Head: When Attitudes Become Form* in der Kunsthalle Bern und im Stedelijk Museum in Amsterdam. Beginn der Freundschaft mit dem Kurator Ad Petersen (1931–2021). Im Juni Umzug mit seiner Partnerin Monika Müller nach Amsterdam.

1970
Heirat mit Monika Müller. An der Rietveld-Akademie in Amsterdam setzt er sich mit verschiedenen Radiertechniken auseinander. Teilnahme an der Ausstellung *Visualisierte Denkprozesse* im Kunstmuseum Luzern, Teilnahme an Ausstellungen in New York und Tokio.

1971
Mehrmonatiger Aufenthalt in Andalusien und Marokko. Zeichnungen für den Animationsfilm *eben.*

1972
Geburt der Tochter Aimée. Erste museale Einzelausstellung im Kunstmuseum Basel, weitere Station im Cabinet des estampes des Musée d'art et d'histoire, Genf. Teilnahme an der documenta 5 in Kassel.

1973
Ausstellung im Goethe-Institut in Amsterdam. Im Sommer Aufenthalt in Carona im Tessin, lernt Meret Oppenheim (1913–1985) kennen.

1974
Anamorphotische Rauminstallation mit dem Motiv des Kopfes von Micky Maus für die Ausstellung *Planetarium* in der Galerie Toni Gerber, Bern.

1975
Aufenthalt in Ägypten und in Tunesien. Teilnahme an Harald Szeemanns Ausstellung *Junggesellenmaschinen* in der Kunsthalle Bern, weitere Stationen in Italien, Belgien, Deutschland, Frankreich, Schweden, Holland und Österreich. Einzelausstellung im Kunsthaus Zürich.

1976
Rückkehr von Carona nach Bern.

1977
Brand des Ateliers an der Neugasse, Verlust zahlreicher Werke. Einzelausstellungen in der Kunsthalle und im Kunstmuseum Bern. Herausgabe des Künstlerbuches *& u. & + &* mit seinen Freunden Walo von Fellenberg und Rolf Geissbühler. Jürgen Glaesemer publiziert die erste grosse Monografie zu Raetz' Zeichnungen. Teilnahme an der Bienal de São Paulo. Beginn der Zusammenarbeit mit dem Kupferdrucker Peter Kneubühler (1944–1999) in Zürich.

1978
Bezug des Ateliers an der Sandrainstrasse 3 in Bern. Bis 2010 jährliche Aufenthalte im Frühling und Herbst in Ramatuelle.

1979
Atelier in Amsterdam als Gast des Stedelijk Museum, in dem er eine Einzelausstellung erhält.

1981
Einzelausstellung im Aargauer Kunsthaus, Aarau, weitere Stationen in Innsbruck und Wien. Aufenthalt in Berlin als Gast des Deutschen Akademischen Austauschdiensts DAAD bis 1982.

1982
Einzelausstellungen in der DAAD-Galerie, Berlin, und in der Kunsthalle Basel. Teilnahme an der documenta 7 in Kassel. Installation einer grossen *MIMI*-Skulptur aus

1983
Whole-room installation at the Kunstmuseum Bern.

1984
"Kunst am Bau" project for the Hofwil teacher-training college and large anamorphic head sculpture made of limestone blocks for the exhibition *Skulptur im 20. Jahrhundert* in the Merian Gardens, Basel.

1985
Large *MIMI* sculpture in stone, Domaine de Kerguehénnec (Brittany). Anamorphic mirror installation *Vue* in the Parc Lullin, Genthod, near Geneva. In summer, produces the first versions of *Zeemansblik*.

1986
First major retrospective at the Kunsthaus Zürich, with further stops in Stockholm and Cologne.

1987
Produces the first versions of the *Feldstechermann* group.

1988
Represents Switzerland at the 43rd Venice Biennale. Solo exhibition at the New Museum of Contemporary Art, New York. Prizewinner at the Trienniale für Originalgrafik, Grenchen.

1989
Solo show at the Museum für Gegenwartskunst, Basel, featuring several *Zeemansblik* reliefs. *Zeemansblik* is also the title of a room in the exhibition.

1990
The bronze plaque *Verlorenes Profil* is erected in front of the Neues Museum, Biel, as a homage to the poet Robert Walser (1878–1956). Solo exhibition at the Museum of Contemporary Art, La Jolla, San Diego (California). Markus Raetz moves into a new studio in a converted orangery on Laubeggstrasse in Bern.

1991
Prix de la Banque hypothècaire du Canton de Genève (BCG prize).

1992
Large *MIMI* sculpture made of wood in a housing estate on rue Damrémont, Paris. Metamorphic head sculpture for the outdoor space outside the extension building at Büelrain cantonal school, Winterthur. As part of Artscape Nordland, a metamorphic cast-iron head is erected on Vestvågøy in the Lofoten islands, Norway. Solo exhibition of prints at the Kunstmuseum Bern and in the Cabinet des estampes at the Musée d'art et d'histoire, Geneva.

1993
Appointed Chevalier de l'Ordre des arts et des lettres de la République française. Solo exhibition at the IVAM Centre Julio Gonzalez, Valencia, with further stops the following year at the Serpentine Gallery, London, and the Musée Rath, Geneva.

1994
Solo exhibition at the Museum of Contemporary Art KIASMA, Helsinki.

2000
The large sculpture *OUI – NON* is erected on the Place du Rhône in Geneva. The Aargauer Kunsthaus, Aarau, acquires the largest *Zeemansblik* relief and a version of the *Feldstechermann* figure in cast iron (*Fernsicht*) for its collection.

2002
Solo exhibition at the Maison Européenne de la Photographie, Paris.

2004
Solo exhibition at the Lindenau Museum, Altenburg (Thuringia), in conjunction with receiving the Gerhard Altenbourg Prize.

2005
Solo exhibition at the Aargauer Kunsthaus, Aarau.

2006
Solo exhibitions at the Carré d'Art – Musée d'art contemporain, Nîmes, and the Museum Moderne Kunst, Salzburg. Prix Meret Oppenheim from the Swiss Federal Office of Culture.

2007
Iwan Schumacher releases his documentary film about Markus Raetz. Raetz becomes a member of the Akademie der Künste, Berlin. Civic medal of the Burgergemeinde Bern.

2012
Solo exhibition of works on paper at the Kunstmuseum Basel.

2014
Rainer Michael Mason publishes the catalogue raisonné of Raetz's prints. Solo exhibition at the Kunstmuseum Bern, with a second stop at the Musée Jenisch, Vevey.

2016
gleich&anders mobile made of embossed aluminum sheet for the stairwell of the extension building at the Bündner Kunstmuseum, Chur. Completion of the hedge maze *Le Palindrome* on a country estate in Jussy, near Geneva. Solo exhibition at the Museo della Svizzera italiana (MASI), Lugano.

2020
Markus Raetz dies on April 14 in Bern.

Granitquadern im Parc de la Cerisaie, Lyon.

1983
Rauminstallation im Kunstmuseum Bern.

1984
Kunst-am-Bau-Projekt für das Lehrerseminar Hofwil und grosse anamorphotische Kopf-Skulptur aus Kalksteinquadern für die Ausstellung *Skulptur im 20. Jahrhundert* in den Merian Gärten, Basel.

1985
Grosse *MIMI*-Skulptur aus Stein, Domaine de Kerguehénnec (Bretagne). Anamorphotische Spiegelinstallation *Vue* im Parc Lullin, Genthod bei Genf. Im Sommer entstehen die ersten Fassungen von *Zeemansblik*.

1986
Erste umfassende Retrospektive im Kunsthaus Zürich, weitere Stationen in Stockholm und in Köln.

1987
Die ersten Fassungen der *Feldstechermann*-Gruppe entstehen.

1988
Vertritt die Schweiz an der 43. Biennale von Venedig. Einzelausstellung im New Museum of Contemporary Art, New York. Preis der Triennale für Originalgrafik, Grenchen.

1989
Einzelausstellung im Museum für Gegenwartskunst, Basel, mit mehreren Exemplaren von *Zeemansblik. Zeemansblik* ist auch der Titel eines Raumes in der Ausstellung.

1990
Vor dem Neuen Museum, Biel, wird die Bronzetafel *Verlorenes Profil* als Hommage für den Dichter Robert Walser (1878–1956) aufgestellt. Einzelausstellung im Museum of Contemporary Art, La Jolla, San Diego (Kalifornien). Markus Raetz bezieht ein neues Atelier in einer ausgebauten Orangerie an der Laubeggstrasse in Bern.

1991
Prix de la Banque hypothècaire des Kantons Genf.

1992
Grosse *MIMI*-Skulptur aus Holz in einer Wohnsiedlung, Rue Damrémont, Paris. Metamorphe Kopf-Skulptur für den Aussenraum des Erweiterungsbaus der Kantonsschule Büelrain, Winterthur. Auf der norwegischen Lofoten-Insel Vestvagoy wird im Rahmen von Artscape Nordland ein metamorpher Kopf aus Eisenguss aufgestellt. Einzelausstellung zum druckgrafischen Werk im Kunstmuseum Bern und im Cabinet des estampes des Musée d'art et d'hisoire, Genf.

1993
Ernennung zum Chevalier de l'Ordre des arts et des lettres de la République française. Einzelausstellung im IVAM Centre Julio Gonzalez, València, weitere Stationen im Folgejahr in der Serpentine Gallery, London, und im Musée Rath, Genf.

1994
Einzelausstellung im Museum of Contemporary Art KIASMA, Helsinki.

2000
Die grosse Skulptur *OUI – NON* wird auf der Place du Rhône in Genf aufgestellt. Das Aargauer Kunsthaus, Aarau, erwirbt die grösste Fassung von *Zeemansblik* sowie ein Exemplar der *Feldstechermann*-Figur in Eisenguss (*Fernsicht*) für seine Sammlung.

2002
Einzelausstellung in der Maison Européenne de la Photographie, Paris.

2004
Einzelausstellung im Lindenau-Museum, Altenburg (Thüringen), im Zusammenhang mit der Verleihung des Gerhard-Altenbourg-Preises an ihn.

2005
Einzelausstellung im Aargauer Kunsthaus, Aarau.

2006
Einzelausstellungen im Carré d'Art, Musée d'art contemporain de Nîmes und im Museum Moderne Kunst, Salzburg.
Prix Meret Oppenheim des Bundesamtes für Kultur.

2007
Iwan Schumacher veröffentlicht seinen Dokumentarfilm über Markus Raetz. Raetz wird Mitglied der Akademie der Künste, Berlin. Medaille der Burgergemeinde, Bern.

2012
Einzelausstellung zu seinem zeichnerischen Werk im Kunstmuseum Basel.

2014
Rainer Michael Mason publiziert den *Catalogue raisonné* des druckgrafischen Werks von Raetz. Einzelausstellung im Kunstmuseum Bern mit einer weiteren Station im Musée Jenisch, Vevey.

2016
Mobile *gleich&anders* aus getriebenem Aluminiumblech für das Treppenhaus im Erweiterungsbau des Bündner Kunstmuseums, Chur. Fertigstellung des Heckenlabyrinths *Le Palindrome* auf einem Landgut in Jussy bei Genf. Einzelausstellung im Museo della Svizzera italiana (MASI), Lugano.

2020
Markus Raetz stirbt am 14. April in Bern.

Contents

Inhalt

Bildnachweis / Image Credits

Umschlag / Cover:
Zeemansblik, 1987
Zinkblech, gefalzt, rückseitige Aufhängevorrichtung: Holz / Zinc sheet, folded, rear-mounted hanging fixture: wood, 83 × 134 × 4,4 cm, 0,1 cm (Stärke Blech / sheet thickness)
Aargauer Kunsthaus, Aarau

Frontispiz / Frontispiece:
Ad Peterson, Portrait von / of Markus Raetz, 1991

Umschlag / Cover:
Aargauer Kunsthaus, Aarau

Frontispiz / Frontispiece:
© Estate Ad Peters

Abb. / Fig. 1:
Zur Verfügung gestellt von Aargauer Kunsthaus Aarau, Foto: Jörg Müller

Abb. / Figs. 3, 8, 13, 14, 18, 19, 24, 25, 32, 36, 39, 41:
SIK-ISEA, Zürich, Alexander Jaquemet, Erlach

Abb. / Fig. 4:
© Max Matter, Aargauer Kunsthaus Aarau, Foto: Jörg Müller

Abb. / Fig. 5:
© Michel Grillet, Aargauer Kunsthaus Aarau, Schenkung Michel und Raffaella Grillet, Foto: SIK-ISEA, Zürich, Phillip Hitz

Abb. / Fig. 6:
© Gaspare Otto Melcher

Abb. / Figs. 7, 12, 15, 31, 33, 35, 38:
SIK-ISEA, Zürich (Philipp Hitz)

Abb. / Fig. 9:
SIK-ISEA, Zürich, Peter Lauri, Bern

Abb. / Fig. 10:
The Louise and Walter Arensberg Collection, 1950-134-75a--e © Association Marcel Duchamp / 2025, ProLitteris, Zurich

Abb. / Fig. 11:
© 2025 Museum Associates / LACMA. Licensed by Art Resource, NY / 2025, ProLitteris, Zurich

Abb. / Fig. 16:
SIK-ISEA, Zürich, Pierre Golendorf, Paris

Abb. / Fig. 17:
SIK-ISEA, Zürich, Markus Raetz, Bern

Abb. / Figs. 23, 28, 29:
SIK-ISEA, Zürich, Nachlass Markus Raetz, Bern

Abb. / Fig. 27:
© Gerhard Richter 2025 (0096)

Abb. / Fig. 34:
SIK-ISEA, Zürich, Thomas Wey, Bern

Abb. / Fig. 37:
Aargauer Kunsthaus Aarau, René Rötheli

Abb. / Fig. 40:
SIK-ISEA, Zürich, Balthasar Burkhard, Bern

Abb. / Fig. 42:
Aargauer Kunsthaus Aarau, Alexandra Roth

Abb. / Fig. 43:
Zur Verfügung gestellt von Kunstmuseum Bern, Rolf Siegenthaler

Impressum / Imprint

Schlüsselwerke der Schweizer Kunst / Landmarks of Swiss Art
Herausgegeben von / Edited by
Angelika Affentranger-Kirchrath

Die Publikation wurde von verschiedenen Seiten grosszügig unterstützt. Dafür danken die Herausgeberin und der Verlag sehr herzlich folgenden Institutionen /
The publication was generously supported by various parties. The editor and Scheidegger & Spiess would like to thank the following institutions for their support:

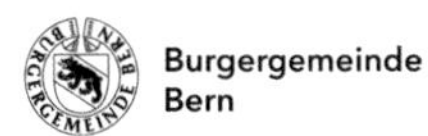

SWISSLOS
Culture Canton de Berne

Ruth & Arthur Scherbarth Stiftung
Gemeinde Büren an der Aare
sowie Stiftungen, die nicht genannt werden möchten / and foundations who do not wish to be named

Übersetzung / Translations: Karen Williams
Lektorat Deutsch: Maike Kleihauer
Copyediting English: Sarah Quigley
Korrektorat Deutsch: Sandra Leitte
Proofreading English: Colette Forder
Projektleitung / Project management:
Anthonie de Groot und / and Chris Reding
Gestaltung / Design: Arturo Andreani,
Visuelle Gestaltung, Bern
Lithografie / Lithography: Martin Flepp,
communicaziun.ch, Chur
Druck und Bindung / Printing and binding:
gugler* DruckSinn, Melk/Donau,
Österreich / Austria

Verlag Scheidegger & Spiess
Niederdorfstrasse 54
8001 Zürich
Schweiz / Switzerland
www.scheidegger-spiess.ch

Der Verlag Scheidegger & Spiess wird vom Bundesamt für Kultur mit einem Strukturbeitrag für die Jahre 2021–2025 unterstützt.

Scheidegger & Spiess is being supported by the Federal Office of Culture with a general subsidy for the years 2021–2025.

ISBN 978-3-03942-242-5